Mennonite
Quilts
and Pieces

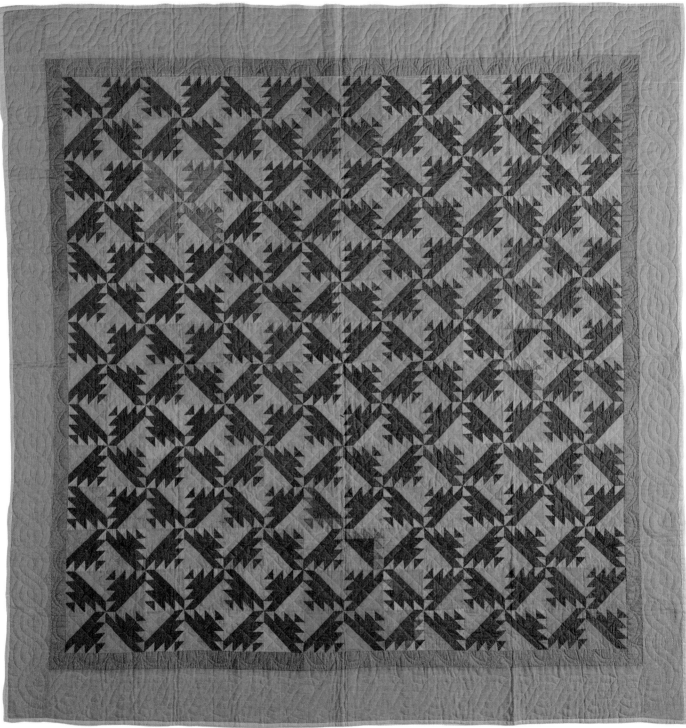

Waves of the Sea, c. 1950
Cotton, 81 × 80
Original quiltmaker: Mattie Nissley Keim
Owner: Emma Keim, Haven
Old Order Amish

Mennonite
Quilts
and Pieces

Judy Schroeder Tomlonson

Good Books
Intercourse, Pennsylvania 17534

Acknowledgments

THANKS to my husband Jim for his constant support, and for my family's encouragement, all of which made the book feasible.

THANKS to all the Amish and Mennonite women and men who talked with me, pulled their treasured quilts out of trunks and off beds to share with all of us, and willingly spoke about themselves and their beliefs and practices.

THANKS to my grandmother and my parents, who have so many stories and enjoy telling them.

THANKS to Mark Wiens, who photographed the quilts with such care, to Robert Regier and to Carol Duerksen, both of whose exquisite photographs caught the beauty of Kansas—all of whom share my General Conference heritage.

And THANKS to Melanie Zuercher and Merle Good for their guidance and encouragement, and for becoming friends in the process.

Design by Craig N. Heisey.

All Scripture quotations are taken from the King James Version of the Bible.

Photograph Credits

Cover photos: Carpenter's Wheel (front) and One-patch (back) quilts: Edwards Photographic, Wichita, Kansas; woman quilting (front): David Kreider; additional scenics (front and back): Robert Regier.

All photos throughout the book were taken by Edwards Photographic, Wichita, Kansas, except the following:
Robert Regier, 5, 8, 12, 17, 20, 28, 31, 32, 55, 59, 60, 64, 68, 71, 72, 76, 78, 87, 88, 93, 94; Carol Duerksen, 14, 40, 46, 48, 51; David Kreider, 80, 95; Judy Tomlonson, 23; Jerry Schmidt, 96.

MENNONITE QUILTS AND PIECES
Copyright © 1985 by Good Books, Intercourse, PA 17534
International Standard Book Number: 0-934672-27-X
Library of Congress Catalog Card Number: 85-070282

Mennonite
Quilts
and Pieces

Table of Contents

Star of the East, c. 1880
Cotton, 84 × 84
Original quiltmaker: a Mrs. Bontrager
Owners: Oren and Mary Ely, Inman
Inman, General Conference Mennonite

A Thing of Beauty

This quilt was made by my mother, who died when I was two, so it is very precious. Later, I remember my stepmother and us girls making quilts, going to quiltings frequently. We each had four quilts when we left home and I still use a quilt on the bed every day. I think most of us do.

Variable Star, c. 1895
Cotton, 72 × 80
Original quiltmaker: Elizabeth Mast Nisly
Owner: Edna Nisly Yoder, Hutchinson
Plainview, Conservative Mennonite

When the Mennonite groups arrived in Kansas in the late 1800s, they were greeted by plains covered with prairie grasses so tall that children could easily get lost in them. Many newly-arrived Mennonite immigrant women cried when they first saw their new homes. They longed for the familiar, for friends and even for trees.

While initially finding shelter in the immigrant barracks provided by the Santa Fe Railroad, which had encouraged them to come to Kansas, Mennonites soon began constructing their first homes. Usually these were just huts. Snow drifted in through the cracks onto the family as they slept. Mothers kept their children in bed for warmth during the day, fearing they would become ill and die. Mennonites finally built permanent homes out of adobe—mud mixed with straw and made into bricks, placed together and plastered with more mud.

Beauty was so absent from the early pioneers' daily lives that they rejoiced when they discovered some. Jacob Schmidt, a Russian Mennonite immigrant, made a note in his diary on April 19, 1875: "Found a little white flower today."

Life was so harsh and austere that the spirits of pioneer women demanded some color and beauty. My grandmother tells of whitewashing adobe walls and using laundry blueing to dab designs around the ceilings and openings, just to bring color into the plain, drab rooms. Quilts were of course born out of economic necessity, but the arrangement of colors satisfied this craving for beauty, and the lack of color in their surroundings intensified the women's appreciation for it.

Mennonites, and certainly the Amish, have always been viewed as being restrained, reserved, and disciplined. Surprisingly, out of what seems a somber life, both inward and out, has emerged quilts so visually dramatic that they resemble modern paintings, particularly those by Kenneth Noland.

Many of the quilts, of course, had blacks, browns and navy, because of the plain, dark clothing which provided the scraps, but also included more colorful pieces from dresses and shirts. Sometimes quiltmakers would purchase a specific color from a travelling peddler, who might make the trip from the large Amish settlement in Shipshewana, Indiana.

Some Mennonites looked at their way of life—farming—as being instituted by God, and at themselves as stewards of His creation. Thus, they had great appreciation for that creation. Flowers, trees and other aspects of nature found their way into quilt designs. Literal representations of flowers were often seen in appliquéd quilts, made as praise offerings to God.

Many Mennonites did not arrive in the U.S. or Kansas until 1874, and, interestingly, quilting had not been a part of their experience. After the turn of the century, through acquaintance with their "English" (non-German-speaking) neighbors, Mennonite women learned the art of quilting. These Russian Mennonites considered the plain quilt in particular to be most beautiful and desirable. They made everyday quilts from scraps, but the Sunday quilt was made from whole cloth. They exhibited their most lavish and minute stitching on a plain quilt—the most elaborately stitched plain quilts appear among the Amish.

Today many quiltmakers still prefer the plain cloth quilt, and most often stitch in a flower design. The sunflower, the Kansas state flower, is a favorite, as is a new pattern appearing in more recent quilts, shafts of wheat in the center with a border of wheatheads. Kansas quiltmakers usually feel there is nothing more lovely than a field of golden wheat with the southern

My mother really liked color, and you could especially see that in the quilts she made. I think, because the times could be so hard, the colors brightened up her world.

Snail Trail, 1958
Cotton, 77 × 89
Original quiltmaker: Minnie Miller Roth
Owner: Opal Roth Lichti, Hesston
Hesston College, Mennonite Church

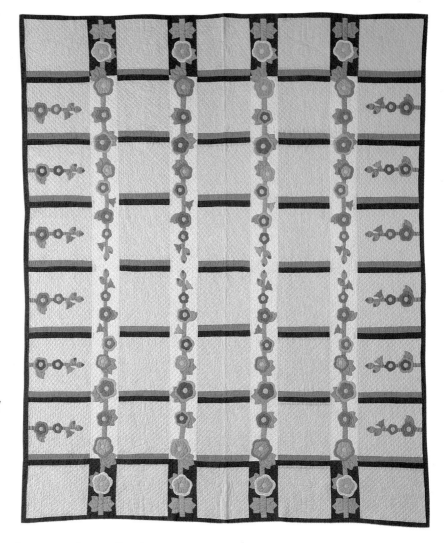

I made this quilt for my hope chest. Back then, girls would make pretty things to put in cedar chests, and hope to get married someday.

Mother always had hollyhocks in her flower garden, and I loved them. This inspired me to make this quilt. The pattern came from the back of a Mountain Mist cotton batting wrapper. My relatives helped me quilt it.

breeze gently rippling it.

When Kansas Mennonites hear critical remarks about their state, they often fail to understand them. There is nowhere else they'd rather live. They tell of how glorious the sunsets are and what a quiet summer evening is like with a mourning dove singing plaintively and the sound of a tractor in the distance as a farmer finishes the day. They continue to feel "the earth is the Lord's and the fullness thereof," and they are being permitted to enjoy it for awhile.

This love of beauty in nature inspired Mennonite housewives in the early days to grow flowers as well as the food they needed to survive. Even today, almost every Mennonite home has flowers in the garden and planted by the front door. Huge flowerbeds, profuse with color, are common, especially around Kansas Amish homes.

(And men aren't immune to the well-tended green beauty of the fields. Many fathers find it difficult to let their children plant the corn, because they take great pride in getting the rows perfectly straight. They claim a talent, usually gained through practice, for sighting that first row to be planted.)

How did the Amish quilts in particular, with their explosions of color, develop? Because quiltmakers had only limited interaction with and exposure to "the world" until about 40 years ago, they were not "contaminated" by contemporary color sense. Amish women chose the colors they liked in

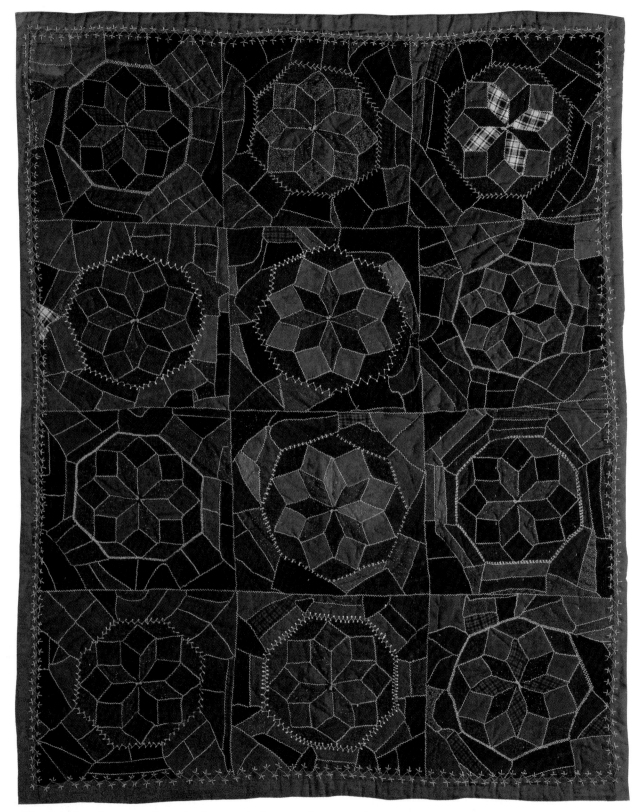

My grandmother must have had an artistic sense because she always chose colors well and liked to make designs in her comforts. We'd save material and give it to her.

Grandmother was such a hard worker and always busy. I never remember her being down about anything—she had such a positive attitude.

Center Star Crazy Patch, 1910
Cotton, 72 × 88
Original quiltmaker: Helena Funk Schmidt
Owner: Ruth Schmidt Unruh, Newton, Kansas
Goessel, General Conference Mennonite

the arrangements they liked. If it was pleasing to their eyes, it was good.

A quilt often reflected the economic status of the quiltmaker—she used what she had—but it also became her method of expressing her individuality, her own sense of color and design. The Mennonite and Amish quilters ultimately used their quilts as an artist would use the canvas, applying colors with patches as an artist would with a brush. The quilter likely received as much satisfaction as the artist did.

Three aspects of quilting remain true for the Amish and for several branches of the Mennonites. First, a quilt is functional. It might only be used on Sundays, but it serves a purpose and is not a frivolous piece of property.

A quilt also allows the expression of an artistic spirit which even yet is not encouraged except in the more liberal branches, such as the General Conference Mennonite, the Mennonite Brethren, and the Mennonite Church.

And a quilt provides a sense of permanency. So much of what is traditionally seen as "women's work" has no lasting value. Washing dishes and making beds may be done again and again, but a quilt is different. A quilt demonstrating love and beauty will be there for years—"A thing of beauty is a joy forever."

Where I grew up, I remember one Sunday morning the old minister gave us a fire and brimstone sermon about showing off our quilts. He disapproved of it and you knew it. But what would have been the incentive if you couldn't be proud of them? It's an accomplishment.
—*Hesston College (Mennonite Church)*

Quilting is the functional part of putting colors and patterns together. It is our art.
—*Lone Tree (Holdeman)*

Leah was a maiden lady who lived with her mother on the farm and milked cows. She didn't lead a very exciting life so maybe she expressed herself in quilting. She died when she was 87 and this is a quilt I inherited from her.

Honey Bee variation, c. 1920
Cotton, 80 × 95
Original quiltmaker: probably Leah Wagler
Owner: Esther Krenzin Wagler, Hutchinson
Sterling, Evangelical Mennonite

Art among the early Mennonites was definitely a thing of necessity. That is the reason the quilts became an art form, because they could use them. A picture on the wall was not useful. Everything was sewed at home, the dresses, the shirts, and there were a lot of scraps. If you made what was pretty besides, it provided a bonus of pleasure.
      —McPherson
      (General Conference Mennonite)

Mother said she was a little girl when she and her mother made this quilt. I have never used it so it is still in perfect shape.

Harvest Sun, 1900
Cotton, 69 × 84
Original quiltmaker: Leah Oyer Krenzin
Owner: Esther Krenzin Wagler, Hutchinson
Sterling, Evangelical Mennonite

14

My mother made this for me shortly after we were married. She probably bought the material from the peddler who came around from Shipshewana, Indiana. His name was Borskey. I do know we bought the blue for my wedding dress from him.

Log Cabin (Barnraising variation), 1930
Cotton, 78 × 88
Original quiltmaker: Betsy Yoder Miller
Owner: Anna Yoder Eash, Haven
Old Order Amish

Peacock Plain, 1935
Cotton sateen, 73 × 87
Original quiltmaker: Suzanne Penner Friesen
Owner: Edna Friesen Reimer, Hesston
Alexanderwohl, General Conference Mennonite

On Sunday you always put on your best, whether it was your good clothes or quilts. Before church, Mother would tell us to make the beds, and on my parents' bed I was to put the "peacock bedspread." Then we were ready for Sunday and for company.

I always liked my parents' bed. It was one of those with the very high headboard. We children liked to stand on the foot of the board and jump off onto the bed, but oh, if we were caught . . . !

Generally, I think it can be said that we Mennonites grew up with the feeling that we should not be too proud. We should not brag, but needlework was okay. On Sunday afternoons, when we went visiting, the ladies would always go to their bedrooms and bring out what they had been working on, tea towels, pillowcases. It was okay to "oh" and "ah" about that. But there was another reason we would show off our handiwork. It was to show that we did not have idle fingers. We had not been sitting around—we had been working and using our time well.
     —*Lehigh (General Conference Mennonite)*

If you paint a picture to hang on the wall, it is like you are asking for a pat on the back. We make what is useful, worthwhile.
     —*Gospel (Holdeman)*

Quilting was a creative expression that we didn't have elsewhere. At least that is true for us who are of Amish background. It was our outlet.
     —*Whitestone (Mennonite Church)*

Waste Not, Want Not

Mennonites could not, and often still cannot, bear to see waste of any kind. During the late 1950s, there was a dress factory at Hillsboro. My mother used scraps from that factory to make this quilt. The size of the scraps determined the size of the pieces. Looking at the arrangement of colors, the reason for the name of the quilt is very evident—the geese are flying in formation.

Flying Geese, 1960
Cotton, 74 × 100
Original quiltmaker: Cornelia "Nellie" Friesen Epp
Owner: Sara Epp Plenert, Lehigh
Lehigh, General Conference Mennonite

Because of persecution, Mennonites had to move often in their 460-year history, trying to find a new homeland where they could practice their faith unmolested. Perhaps because of this continual "starting over," frugality became a distinct way of life for the Mennonites and Amish.

Whatever its basis, frugality is considered an integral part of stewardship and trying to live the simple life. Wasting anything is considered irresponsible—almost a sin. You do not waste what God has provided.

Proverbs 6:6, "Go to the ant, thou sluggard; consider her ways, and be wise," reinforced frugality in the older generation. So did an oft-repeated "English" saying: "Use it up; wear it out; make it do or do without."

When they homesteaded in Kansas, Mennonites were required to plant trees. Many times, they planted Osage orange trees to mark the boundary lines. These trees served the Mennonite concept of frugality perfectly. They made hedge posts from the wood—they outlasted any other kind of posts, surviving as long as 60 years. Housewives declared that anything made by God had to have a purpose and was not to be wasted—women still use the inedible Osage orange "fruit" by placing these "hedge apples" at doorways and window wells to prevent the annoying, chirping crickets from coming inside in the fall.

Quilting also provides a perfect medium for celebrating frugality, by using scraps. Many Mennonite quilters find it inconsistent with their theology to buy coordinated fabric just to cut it up and piece it back together again. Instead, they will save scraps from family sewing, sharing and trading scraps with relatives and neighbors to get the colors they need. When the scraps are used for one quilt pattern, the remaining smaller scraps are cut for a Postage Stamp or tiny Flower Garden quilt. Not a single piece is to be wasted.

A generation ago, it was absolutely necessary to have a scrap bag and a rag bag. When all the good pieces of material were cut from the old clothing, only then did it become a rag. One quilt within the General Conference church has scraps from 36 different dresses and blouses, a housecoat and the bedroom curtains—and some of those pieces are pieced.

Sometimes remaining rags were sewed into strips and made into rag rugs, still seen on the shiny hardwood floors of Amish and some Mennonite homes. Today, even plastic bread bags, which some women find very hard to discard, are made into throw rugs.

Years ago, especially during the Depression and into the 1950s, it was necessary for each family to use what it had on hand. This meant using flour, sugar and salt sacks, which had printing on them, for clothing. On some quilts, the printing is still visible. Feed sacks with colorful prints provided dress material and scraps for quilts.

Many older Mennonites are concerned that each succeeding generation is becoming less careful about frugality and a simple life. A woman tells a story about her grandmother, whose daughter made her a new "everyday" dress. At first, the grandmother wore that dress to church because she did not want to "waste" the new for work. New was special and it belonged in church. While this is the extreme in simple living, often the concern about waste is no longer there, and many Mennonites and Amish regret it.

There isn't a single block in here that is like another. We call it a Beggar's Quilt because my sister, Ina Krenzin, and I begged scraps from our neighbors or anyone we thought would have some scraps. I pieced this quilt with the help of my grandmother, Anna Oyer, of Abbyville, Kansas. She quilted it. She always did lots of quilting for neighbors or anyone who wanted quilting done.

Tumbling Blocks, c. 1930
Cotton, 85 × 87
Original quiltmaker: owner
*Owner: Esther Krenzin Wagler, Hutchinson
Sterling, Evangelical Mennonite*

21

Broken Star, 1981
Tricot, 93 × 103
Original quiltmakers: Frieda and Barbara
Nisly Yoder
Owner: Frieda Yoder, Hutchinson
Beachy Amish

There is a lingerie factory in Iowa where we have relatives who gathered and gave us the scraps from the dump to make this quilt. They used to be able to get in free but I think now you have to pay a dollar to gather the scraps. My daughter and I pieced the quilt and friends helped quilt it.

Mother used what she had, feed sacks. At that time you just didn't go out and buy new material. She embroidered a design in the center and added pieces of green scraps and then quilted it with green crochet thread. This really is a bedspread because we didn't use any batting.

Each of my four sisters had a quilt like this but used pink instead. Mother had already made a pink quilt for me, so I asked for green.

Embroidered feed sack, 1951
Cotton, 86 × 88
Original quiltmaker: Edna Nisly Yoder
Owner: Bertie Yoder Miller, Hutchinson
Plainview, Conservative Mennonite

23

Crazy Patch, 1915
Upholstery fabric, 70 × 81
Original quiltmaker: Mary Albrecht Zimmerman
Owner: Phyllis Alber Rinehart, Plevna
Sterling, Evangelical Mennonite

This comfort is extremely heavy because it is made of upholstery fabrics. You used to be able to buy sample books and our parents couldn't stand to see that material go to waste, so it was used. Because it is so heavy, we have laughingly decided that when you were lying in bed and decided you wanted to change positions, you'd have to say, "Lift. One, two, three, turn," and then lower the comfort again.

We haven't been able to figure out how it was tacked. You can't find a knot on top or on the bottom.

Letha's Electric Fan, 1939
Cotton, 92 × 94
Original quiltmaker: owner
Owner: Anna Koehn, Moundridge
Gospel, Holdeman

I found this pattern in the Kansas City Star, *dated April 28, 1938, and liked the pattern so much that I made the quilt, long before we had electricity. The scraps came from the family sewing.*

Brick Work, c. 1960
Whipped cream, 90 × 103
Original quiltmakers: Marie Loewen Jost (pieced)
        LuElla Reimer Jost (quilted)
Owner: LuElla Reimer Jost, Hillsboro
Parkview, Mennonite Brethren

We caught more than fish on a fishing trip to Minnesota. My cousin had some whipped cream quilt blocks she didn't know what to do with, and gave them to me. I asked Marie to piece them together and she designed the way they are placed.

A Family of Faith

Mission sales have always been an important way to raise money for relief and the support of our missionaries. My parents bought this quilt at a sale in South Dakota, and it may have been made by a friend of my mother's. When we divided her things, it became ours.

Broken Star, c. 1945
Cotton, 82 × 82
Original quiltmaker: unknown
Owner: Mary Kroeker Loewen, Hillsboro
Ebenfeld, Mennonite Brethren

27

"True evangelical faith cannot lie dormant. It feeds the hungry, it clothes the naked, it comforts the sorrowful, it shelters the destitute, it serves those that harm it, it binds up that which is wounded, it has become all things to all men."

—*Menno Simons*

Practicing the above belief is probably the most unifying aspect for all the Mennonite groups in Kansas. They are a caring and sharing people. This was true in the past, when each individual church would have its own mission sale to support missionaries or relief projects, and is still true today.

Who are these people who believe that faith and love are action verbs?

The Mennonites originated in Switzerland as a part of the Protestant Reformation in the 16th century. A small group of believers became convinced the reforms of Martin Luther and Ulrich Zwingli had not gone far enough. This group was nicknamed "Anabaptists," meaning "rebaptizers." Anabaptists believed infant baptism was wrong because a child was not aware of its sin—only a believing adult was capable of deciding to repent and be baptized.

Consequently, the Anabaptists preached against a state church, which required everyone to be members, and argued for a church where persons could *voluntarily* choose membership upon confession of faith and baptism. This was a revolutionary concept.

On January 21, 1525, three persons—Felix Manz, Conrad Grebel

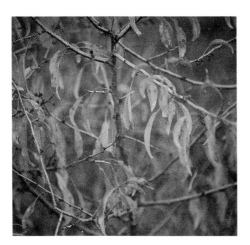

Shoofly, 1921
Cotton, 87 × 98
Original quiltmaker: Susie Warkentin Unruh
Owner: Velma Unruh Franz, Newton
Alexanderwohl, General Conference Mennonite

My father [P. H. Unruh] went to help distribute food and clothing, gathered from Mennonites in the U.S., to Mennonites and non-Mennonites who were suffering so terribly [in Russia in 1921]. He was gone for over six months. I remember I was in the fourth grade, and it was during this time that my mother did an awful lot of quilting. This quilt was made during that time.

She was the president of the first sewing society at Alexanderwohl, where my father was pastor for 38 years. The ladies would come to our house to quilt and tie comforts that were always given away to the needy. We would set up the frame in the parlor. My mother was always a lady who was very willing to help everyone.

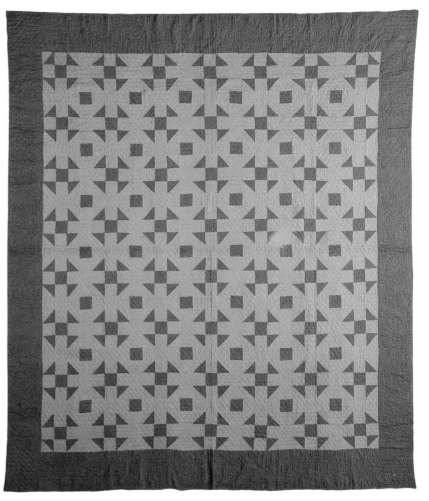

This quilt was given to us by my mother-in-law as a wedding present. Born in Russia December 23, 1867, she came to the United States with her parents at the age of six and settled in Indiana. They later moved to Reno County, Kansas, where she raised five children.

Cleveland Lilies, c. 1930
Cotton, 67 × 76
Original quiltmaker: Katie Albrecht Roth
Owner: Mollie Wagner Roth, Sterling
Sterling, Evangelical Mennonite

29

Hexagon, c. 1880
Cotton, 68 × 82
Original quiltmaker: a Mrs. Bontrager
Owners: Oren and Mary Ely, Inman
Inman, General Conference Mennonite

Often, within the Mennonite church, quilts would find their way into other branches than where they originated. Such is the case of this quilt. It was originally made by an Amish woman, a Mrs. Bontrager, over 100 years ago. It is said of her that she enjoyed smoking a pipe and would often do so after dinner.

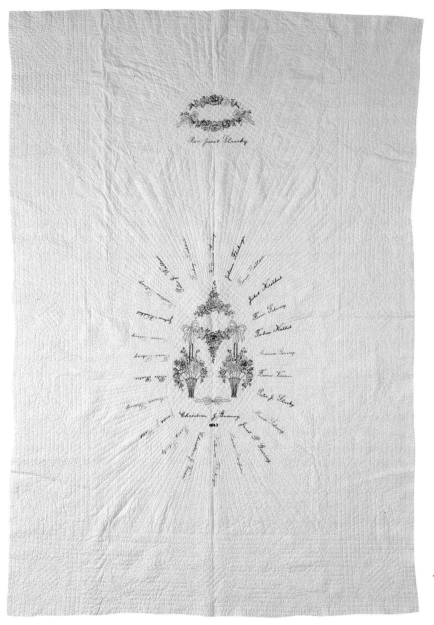

Baptismal quilt, c. 1940
Cotton, 69 × 97
Original quiltmaker: Anna Grader Goering
Owner: Helen Goering Goering, Moundridge
Eden, General Conference Mennonite

My father, C. J. Goering, who became a minister, and my mother were baptized in South Dakota in 1896. Years later, they decided to each make a baptismal quilt. They used the old copper boiler to determine the size of the center design with flower baskets filling the area. My father wrote the names of the class members and Mother did the embroidery. This is my father's quilt.

and Georg Blaurock—baptized each other, beginning the "Swiss Brethren." Deviation from the state church was not tolerated, however, and within four years all the original leaders were dead.

Despite the severe persecution (over 4,000 men and women died gruesome martyrs' deaths), the movement spread rapidly through Switzerland to Germany, France and The Netherlands, where a parish priest, Menno Simons, became an ardent supporter in 1536. Through his preaching, debating and writing, Menno helped unify the Swiss Brethren, who eventually became known as Mennonites.

The Mennonites emphasized that love had to be the basis of all social relations—"Love your enemies, bless them that curse you, do good to them that hate you and pray for them who despitefully use you and persecute you" (Matthew 6:44). A favorite story is that of Dirk Willems, an Anabaptist who was being pursued by a sheriff over a frozen lake when the ice broke and the sheriff fell into the water. Willems stopped fleeing to rescue the sheriff, and was arrested and burned at the stake in 1569. All Anabaptist groups continue to practice peace and nonresis-

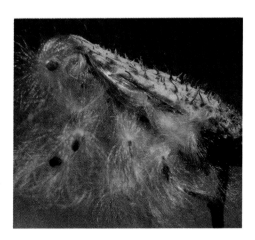

tance in all facets of life. This includes refusal to participate in military service.

The Mennonites needed boundless courage over the next 50 years. Their leaders were almost always killed and they were not allowed to worship publicly. They had no right to own property. As "Defenseless Christians," they refused to fight for their rights, so they were constantly on the move, searching for freedom to practice their faith in peace.

In 1693, a Mennonite minister from France, Jacob Amman, led a difficult, painful split from the Mennonites, a division that sprang from Amman's conviction that the church was getting too lax in enforcing the discipline which kept it from "worldliness." Amman's followers were called Amish. The Amish and Mennonites today are like religious cousins. Their differences are primarily in lifestyle and practices rather than basic beliefs.

Meanwhile, a group of German Mennonites were among the first to settle William Penn's colony in the New World, landing at Germantown, Pennsylvania in 1683. Later, European Mennonites moved to Poland, Prussia and South Russia. Eventually, 50,000 left Russia and came to the Great Plains, and Canada. In 1874, 18,000 Mennonites left Russia for North America, with nearly 5,000 settling in Kansas alone.

What brought so many Mennonites to primarily four counties in central Kansas? Initially, it was cheap land, between $2.50 and $3.00 an acre.

Also, perhaps because continuing persecution had caused Mennonites to move so often, they had developed a spirit of adventure. They often were some of the first settlers to move into newly-opened territories. Kansas was admitted to the Union in 1861. The Homestead Act followed in 1862, and by 1869, Indiana Mennonites had purchased land in Marion County, Kansas.

As land became more expensive and crowded in Lancaster County, Pennsylvania and in Virginia, where large numbers of Mennonites and related groups had settled, the people moved West. Street signs in Hesston, Kansas, today give a good indication of settlers' origins— Weaver, Hess and Herr are all Lancaster County names.

The largest group of Mennonites to settle in Kansas, however, came from Russia and were recruited by the Kansas Land Department and the Santa Fe Railroad. Because of a washed-out bridge in Nebraska, the first Amish group was also encouraged by a railroad agent to look at the area southeast of Hutchinson, instead of Nebraska, where they live to this day.

The Mennonites had left Russia almost en masse in the latter part of the 1800s, when they feared the life they had known there for nearly 100 years was being threatened. In 1870, the conscription law would have required their young men to serve in the army. They would have been forced to give up the German language and their own schools and government. It seemed the only solution was to move again, this time to America.

One hundred and ten years later, some acculturation has of course occurred. But some distinctive features remain. Among these are the place of the Bible as the normative guide for life, the practice of voluntary adult baptism, the separation of church and state, and peace and nonresistance applied to all areas of life. There are other, less broad

Not only were leftover scraps used in making quilts, but the good fabric in worn-out clothes was reused. My Missouri grandmother made this quilt and her sisters made similar quilts from scraps and good material in old Sunday dresses. I received this quilt after the death of my father.

The star in the corner is misconstructed, with the white pieces signalling an obvious error. This error was likely made on purpose. It was a tradition earlier to make an "error" in each quilt because, it was pointed out, "Only God is perfect." These errors were made to demonstrate your humility.

Old Maid's Patience, 1926
Wools and rayons, 69 × 74
Original quiltmaker: Mary Kropf Hershberger
Owner: Pearl Hershberger Rodgers, Hesston
Whitestone, Mennonite Church

Fox and Geese, c. 1967
Cotton, 79 × 88
Original quiltmaker: Clara Stimle Leppke
Owner: Donna Dick Dalke, Hillsboro
Ebenfeld, Mennonite Brethren

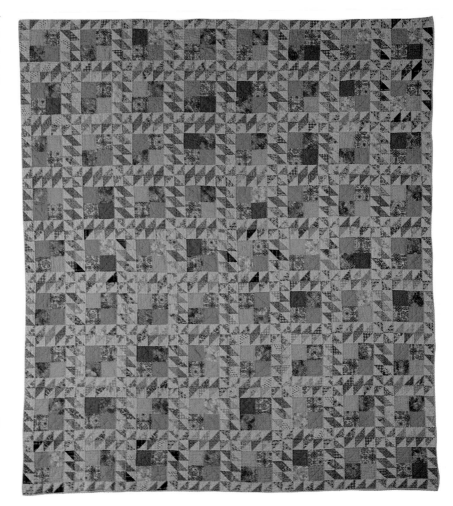

This quilt was a wedding gift from my step-grandmother, who was a professional seamstress. She could make anything and everything and made quilts for all her older grandchildren.

Double Wedding Ring (baby quilt), 1936
Cotton, 36 × 36
Original quiltmaker: Kathryn Hildebrand Klaassen
Owner: Harriet Klaassen Suderman, Hillsboro
Ebenfeld, Mennonite Brethren

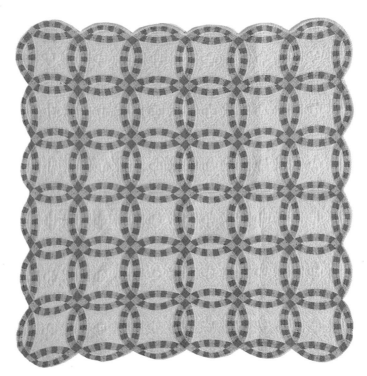

My aunt made this baby quilt for my mother as a gift when I was born, her first child. Can you imagine the patience it took to handpiece those 36 pieces together in each circle, which meant a total of 1,296 pieces? And with all the work that had to be done on their Oklahoma farms in those days.

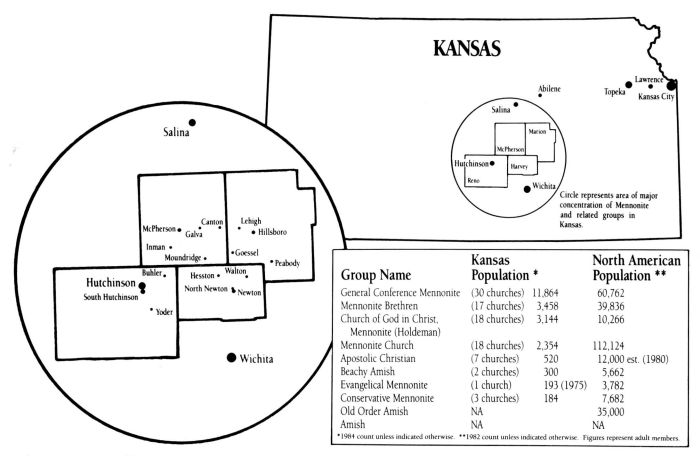

KANSAS

Circle represents area of major concentration of Mennonite and related groups in Kansas.

Group Name	Kansas Population *		North American Population **
General Conference Mennonite	(30 churches)	11,864	60,762
Mennonite Brethren	(17 churches)	3,458	39,836
Church of God in Christ, Mennonite (Holdeman)	(18 churches)	3,144	10,266
Mennonite Church	(18 churches)	2,354	112,124
Apostolic Christian	(7 churches)	520	12,000 est. (1980)
Beachy Amish	(2 churches)	300	5,662
Evangelical Mennonite	(1 church)	193 (1975)	3,782
Conservative Mennonite	(3 churches)	184	7,682
Old Order Amish	NA		35,000
Amish	NA		NA

*1984 count unless indicated otherwise. **1982 count unless indicated otherwise. Figures represent adult members.

distinctives as well.

The family is of utmost importance and held in high esteem. Divorce is far below the national average—nonexistent in some branches. People enjoy family reunions on holidays and other occasions, and tracing genealogies. Mennonites play "The Mennonite Game" at any large gathering—they trace names to "place" a mutual friend or relative. (In a number of churches, the "game" is getting harder to play as churches reach into communities and draw in members with non-Mennonite names. Many members feel this is as it should be if they are faithful to Christ's injunction to "go into all the world and preach the Gospel.")

Among the Kansas Mennonites and Amish, there is much intermarriage, which certainly becomes evident when tracing the history of their quilts. A quilt may have originated in one branch but may be passed on to a member in another. That is particularly true of persons south of Hutchinson, where there are three branches of Amish and another group which originated from the Amish. One immediate family may have members in as many as three different branches. If the theology of a certain branch does not meet spiritual needs, there may be movement to another branch before moving "outside" into a mainstream Protestant group.

Another distinctive feature shared by most Mennonites and Amish is the "tender conscience." Most will refuse to go to war, believing that as servants of Christ they are required to return good for evil. This stand has resulted in a great deal of persecution, even death, through the years. If a young man chooses the military, some branches will automatically excommunicate him. Other branches may allow him to go as a noncombatant. Under the Selective Service Act, large numbers of

Mennonites and Amish young men participated in alternative service, working in hospitals, forestry and health projects and other community services or in agricultural development overseas.

Serving others is so highly stressed by most Mennonites that many young people choose to do voluntary service. Nearly every branch has a way by which their young people, and older persons also, can serve, for several months to as long as three years, usually for no return other than room and board.

Almost all the Mennonite groups—and certainly those in central Kansas—participate in the Mennonite Central Committee (MCC), a relief and service agency. Support takes the form of volunteers in locations all over North America and throughout the world, as well as congregations who can or pack meat or corn, mend, sort and pack used clothing, make lye soap, and provide other material aid for the world's needy. Congregations, especially the women, often make quilts to sell at the MCC Relief Sales, such as the one held in April every year at Hutchinson. The proceeds from these sales go to MCC.

While often outwardly there seems to be much diversity—in dress, transportation, education, use of energy, acceptance of technology, wedding and funeral practices, church services, lifestyle—between the various branches, the common thread is the love of Christ and trying to live faithful lives.

One-patch, c. 1890
Wools and cashmere, 72 × 78
Original quiltmaker: Elizabeth Mast Nisly
Owner: Bertie Yoder Miller, Hutchinson
Plainview, Conservative Mennonite

A surprising amount of red is used in this quilt, which was not typical of the Amish people, where this quilt originated. This particular red, however, was very colorfast.

The Amish women always wore long black dresses and usually their slips weren't that long, so they had very deep hems, as much as ten inches deep. This red material was then used to form the hems rather than use the "good" dress material, all for modesty's sake.

They also had to have highbutton shoes so people wouldn't see their legs, either, but they really needed those shoes in those days for warmth, too.

This quilt is very special because it was made by my grandmother, who died when Mother was two.

Tulip Appliqué, c. 1930
Cotton, 72 × 90
Original quiltmaker: Eva Emch
Owner: Dina Wernle Emch, Madison
Lamont, Apostolic Christian

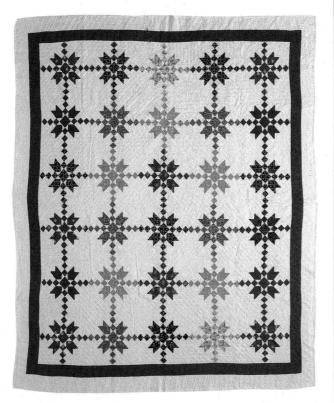

Snowflake, 1894
Cotton, 72 × 90
Original quiltmaker: Elizabeth Zimmerman
Flickinger
Owner: Ruth Flickinger, South Hutchinson
Sterling, Evangelical Mennonite

About the People

In the *MENNONITE CHURCH,* individual congregations vary from being more "open to change" to "conservative." The Mennonite Church emphasizes missions, is quite peace oriented and supports higher education (their junior college is located in Hesston). A number of congregations determine the will of the church through "discernment": reaching consensus after a great deal of prayer. The mode of baptism is often as the individual prefers. Communion is open to all believing Christians. Members are seldom excommunicated. Ministers are called by a congregation for a period of time and are usually seminary-trained and paid. There are a few women pastors, although there is some resistance to them. Stewardship in goods and land is emphasized.

Members of the Mennonite Church drive cars, use modern farm equipment, and have radios, TV and thoroughly modern homes. Dress is not particularly distinctive, though some women, especially older ones, do wear the head covering or "prayer veiling" for church and church functions. They may use musical instruments in their worship services and enjoy and are well-known for their four-part singing.

The *GENERAL CONFERENCE MENNONITE CHURCH,* usually considered the most liberal of the all the branches, began in 1860 when John Oberholtzer and others became concerned that practices were being followed from habit rather than biblical precedent, and that major issues should be decided by the congregations rather than the bishop. "Freedom of conscience" has become the General Conference hallmark. It is a continual struggle, they say, between tradition and wanting to be effective in the world.

The General Conference is mission-minded and has always supported publication (their denominational publishing house is in Newton) and higher education (Bethel College is in North Newton). They do not excommunicate, but try to win the errant back through caring confrontation. They are very peace-oriented and they do vote. Lifestyle, worship practices and the ministry resemble those of the Mennonite Church. Women are more accepted as ministers, and do not wear head coverings.

The *MENNONITE BRETHREN CHURCH,* which began in 1860 during a "spiritual awakening" in Russia, since that time has had a more evangelistic

Single Irish Chain, 1913
Cotton, 67 × 90
Original quiltmaker: Amanda Mast Nisly
Owner: Lydia Nisly Yoder, Partridge
Beachy Amish

My father got this quilt from home when he married. I think the red was used because it didn't fade so easily. We didn't always appreciate quilts like we do now. Old quilts were old quilts. I let my daughter take this quilt to Bible school, then my son used it. Now, I don't know how I let them do that.

Center Diamonds, 1918
Cotton, 68 × 82
Original quiltmaker: Betsy Yoder Yoder
Owner: Susie Schrock Bontrager, Haven
Old Order Amish

About the People

This Amish quilt was made in 1918 by Betsy Yoder Yoder for her step-daughter, Deemy Yoder. It is now owned by Deemy's daughter, Susie Schrock Bontrager. Mrs. Bontrager still has a cranberry red bonnet of the same color that appears in the quilt.

thrust than most other groups. They continue to emphasize missions and "winning souls to the Kingdom." They encourage higher education—Tabor College is located in Hillsboro.

The Bible is interpreted literally. Conversion must precede baptism. The mode is "once backwards" as a symbol of Christ's burial and resurrection. Pastors are trained and called.

Women's roles are traditional, with no women pastors. Homes are modern. They have TVs and radios but often discourage their children from attending movies and dances. They vote, and are not as nonresistant as they once were, with some members serving in the military.

Members of the *CHURCH OF GOD IN CHRIST, MENNONITE,* are usually called Holdemans after their founder, John Holdeman, who separated from the Mennonite Church in 1858, convinced the Mennonites were no longer practicing the faith of Menno Simons, especially church discipline. The Holdemans, and the Amish, are certainly the most disciplined people. They practice excommunication and avoidance, not to punish but to bring the errant back into the church. Ministers are elected for a lifetime of non-paid ministry.

There is no formal dating. Members are led to partners through direction by the Lord, called "conviction." A marriage will take place only after a great deal of prayer. There is no divorce.

Most members consider theirs the "true" church and their primary mission is saving their children's souls. Thus they have their own schools through eighth grade. Persons may seek more education if they have the conviction and permission for training in a service-oriented occupation such as nursing or teaching.

The Holdemans believe that self-denial leads to contentment. They have no TVs, radios or pictures on the walls although they have modern homes. As with the Old Order Amish, no photographs are allowed, as that can lead to pride and vanity.

Women wear modest clothing with black hose; men have beards. The women wrap a black, three-cornered scarf around their bun of hair for everyday and use it to cover their heads, tied under the chin, during worship. It is a symbol of submission to God and to their husbands.

The Holdemans do not vote because they feel it gives elected officials their permission to use force. Entering the mili-

Single Irish Chain, 1978
Polyester cotton, 90 × 99
Original quiltmaker: Katie Beachy Yoder
Owner: Verna Yoder Hershberger,
Hutchinson
Amish

*I made this quilt for Verna
when she got married. Each child got
two quilts.*

Christmas Star, 1934
Cotton, 90 × 72
Original quiltmaker: owner
Owner: Eva Koehn Wedel, Moundridge
Gospel, Holdeman

Friendship Knot, c. 1930
Cotton, 76 × 90
Original quiltmaker: Margaretha Unruh Schroeder
Owners: Rudoph and Eulalia Duerksen
Schroeder, Hillsboro
Alexanderwohl, General Conference Mennonite

About the People

tary means automatic excommunication.

There are three groups of Amish living generally south of Hutchinson. The *OLD ORDER AMISH* are the most conservative, insisting on the most "non-conforming to" and separation from "the world." Because of this, they have, ironically, attracted the world's attention. They wear plain dress; men have beards. They drive horses and buggies and do not have telephones or electricity, although they utilize gas appliances. Many are farmers and families still farm together. Their worship services are conducted in homes, every other week. They do not have Sunday school or participate in missions. Their children attend the public school in Yoder, but not beyond the eighth grade.

The group known simply as *AMISH* is less conservative than the Old Order. They have electricity (but no TVs or radios), telephones, carpeting in many homes, and pictures on the walls. The Amish originally came to Kansas from Illinois because they wanted to be more innovative and conduct Sunday school. They meet in homes every other Sunday for worship; on "off" Sundays, they have Sunday school in the meetinghouse. This building is also used for the sewing society. They drive horses and buggies, and also use their modern farm equipment for transportation.

The *BEACHY AMISH* became distinct from the local Amish in 1958 (although the Beachy church began in Pennsylvania in 1927). Unlike most schisms, the local separation occurred without hard feelings when a number of the Amish became very interested in missions and in owning cars.

The Beachy Amish accept electricity and telephones but not TV or radios. They have their own high school and encourage young people with service-oriented goals to go on with higher education. They wear plain dress, with slight variations. They meet in a church building but have no musical instruments in their worship services. Like many Mennonite groups, they conduct Wednesday evening prayer services.

The *CONSERVATIVE MENNONITE CHURCH* separated from the local Amish in 1948 (nationally became a distinct branch in 1910), also because of interest in Sunday schools and missions.

They stress missions and support work in Central America and parts of the U.S. They wear modified plain and modest modern dress, always with the head covering for women. Their views on education and their worship practices basically follow those of the Beachy Amish. They enjoy four-part singing.

Drunkard's Path, 1945
Cotton, 79 × 87
Original quiltmakers: Mary Kropf Hershberger
(pieced)
Clara Brenneman Hershberger
Owner: Pearl Hershberger Rodgers, Hesston
Whitestone, Mennonite Church

This Drunkard's Path was pieced by my grandmother. My mother, however, did not like all that red, so she took the main blocks apart and put white ones in between, decreasing the red, which then provided enough blocks to make a quilt for myself and my brother Glenn. Mother and some of her relatives and friends quilted both quilts.

Waterlily Plain, 1930
Cotton, 72 × 84
Original quiltmaker: owner
Owner: Ethel Wedel Friesen, Hillsboro
Parkview, Mennonite Brethren

Years ago, when all young ladies waited for Prince Charming to come along, we would prepare for that event by making beautiful embroidered linens and, above all, a few nice quilts. These then would be placed in a cedar chest, usually given to us by our parents.

This quilt was marked by Mrs. A. R. Ebel, whose husband was a professor at Tabor College, with the waterlily design. My mother put in a few stitches, but I took those out without her knowing because my pride was great—I wanted to have all my own even stitches in it. I have used it on my spare bed all these years. When the time comes to pass it on, it shall go to my only granddaughter.

About the People

Conservative Mennonites have modern homes, though without TV (they do have radios), and they drive cars. They do not vote and all civil service is discouraged. They practice excommunication.

All three Amish groups and the Conservative Mennonites choose their ministers by lot, according to Proverbs 16:33: "The lot is cast into the lap; but the whole disposing thereof is of the Lord." The ministry is for a lifetime of service, without pay.

Amish, Beachy Amish and Conservative Mennonite children attend public school at the Elreka school near the rural community of Pleasantview.

The *EVANGELICAL MENNONITE CHURCH* began in 1864 following a deep, personal, religious experience of an Amish bishop, Henry Egli. His followers were called Egli Amish and then Defenseless Mennonites. He charged that people were indifferent to spiritual things and needed to experience a new birth before joining the church through baptism.

In 1948, the church adopted the name Evangelical Mennonite; by implication, evangelism is important. They emphasize missions and outreach into their own community.

They are probably the least traditionally Mennonite of the Kansas groups and probably the best described as fundamentalists. They emphasize personal salvation and not family heritage. Baptismal methods are optional, but no one can become a church member before age 14. Trained ministers are called by the congregations.

Although the *APOSTOLIC CHRISTIAN CHURCH* is not a member of the immediate family of Mennonites, it is a first cousin because many original members were Amish and Mennonites. The Apostolic Christians share many of the same beliefs and participate in joint efforts.

The founder of the church was Samuel Froelich from Brugg, Switzerland, who was expelled from the Reformed Church in 1832. In 1876, members moved to Kansas from Ohio and Illinois, where they felt crowded, looking for cheap land.

Baptism is by immersion, one time backward. Women wear a strip of lace as a headcovering, and modern, modest dress. When drafted, men serve as noncombatants in the military.

It should be noted that Kansas groups across the board are generally more "liberal" than their "eastern" relatives. As pioneer people, they had to depend more on themselves and less on tradition; in some cases, in fact, they created their own.

Hard Work and
Hard Times

Helena's husband Daniel was a first cousin to John Holdeman, the founder of the Church of God in Christ, Mennonite—the Holdeman church. She pieced the quilt all by hand, and it was quilted by my mother. It's called "Missouri Roadside" because the roads in Missouri are so crooked.

Missouri Roadside, 1926
Cotton, 84 × 87
Original quiltmakers: Helena Koehn Holdeman,
Esther Johnson Holdeman
Owner: Betty Holdeman Johnson, Galva
United Center, Holdeman

Quilts are a vivid testimony to the strength of the Amish and Mennonite women of Kansas. They have endured hard, trying times and not only have they survived, but they have created substantial beauty, often out of very little. Life did not defeat them and, perhaps because of the difficulty, the good and the lovely was expressed in the quilts which brightened their world.

Each new season in Kansas would bring its own peril, and still does. The suddenly balmy spring day melted the snow and could inspire torrential rains, flooding crops and homes. The tornado's unleashed fury flattened everything in its path. The summer's blistering heat and angry south winds shriveled the wheat and threatened the fall harvest. A devastating hailstorm could destroy the crops within minutes, even stripping the leaves from the trees. The winter winds blasted the people with bone-chilling temperatures and crippling blizzards.

The Kansas prairies exacted heavy toll from the early settlers. Death came too soon and too easily, and sorrow was almost a constant part of life. One Mennonite family near Goessel buried five children within one year. It is hard to imagine now how they could have survived such pain.

Nature seemed to conspire to test the settler's will, as grasshoppers invaded the land. So many swarmed in, they darkened the sky. When they finally moved on, the grasshoppers had consumed every green living thing, even feeding on wood, the family clothes, curtains and bedding.

Not only did Nature play havoc with the lives of the Mennonites, but society inflicted hard times as well. Many older Mennonites and Amish tell of how difficult it was making ends meet during the Depression. Wheat, the mainstay of the farmer, sold for 26¢ a bushel. Corn was so cheap that instead of selling it, they burned the whole ears for fuel, rather than buy coal.

My mother remembers that when she was 11 years old, she and her sister needed shoes. Her father measured their feet, went to Peabody and bought two pairs of ladies' pointed-toe shoes with two-inch heels for 25¢. The shoes were old and too tight, but they wore them and were very proud of them, besides!

Material sold for 10¢ a yard, and when Mother went to high school, she had only two dresses. She wore one dress one week and the second dress the next. The material was not colorfast and by the end of the school year, both dresses had faded to almost white.

World War II brought more hard times to the Mennonites. Many were ridiculed because of their German language, and their peace position and refusal to participate in military service. A large number of men served in Civilian Public Service or went to the front as noncombatants, often as medics who carried no weapons.

Farming was, and perhaps remains, the hardest way to provide a living for the family, and until the last 25 years, farming was the primary occupation of the Mennonites and Amish. It is estimated that now only 60–65% in Kansas are farmers.

The Kansas wheat harvest was a bone-weary time but it provided a tangible witness to successful farming. The farmer watched the sky and prayed for favorable weather, rubbing the wheathead between his hands each morning to check the moisture content. When harvest began, women and children would take dinner out to the field and

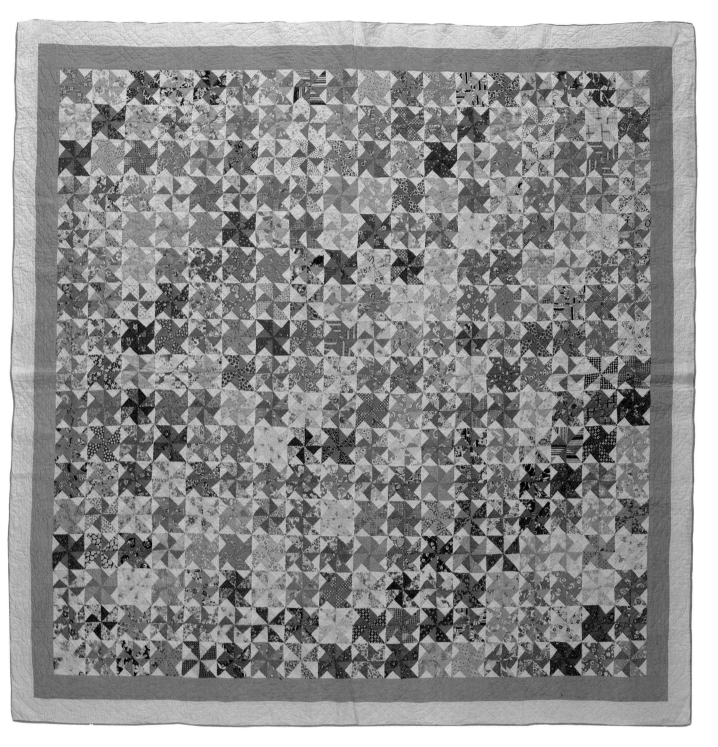

Quilting was a winter activity for my Nebraska grandmother. Piecing was done during the summer in spare moments between chores, gardening and canning and, often, field work for some women.

A scrap quilt doesn't have to look like a scrap quilt. My grandmother tied this quilt together by purchasing the blue for the border and the backing.

This quilt is very special to me because I never got to know my grandmother. She died the very day my parents were married.

Dutchman's Windmill, c 1930
Cotton, 82 × 84
Original quiltmakers: Kathryn Bergen Epp (pieced)
Tina Gaedde Dick (quilted)
Owner: Pat Epp Schmidt, Newton
Alexanderwohl, General Conference Mennonite

My grandmother, who was Amish, made this quilt for her daughter Barbara, who later died. The quilt was then passed on to me.

My grandmother was one whose hands were never idle, even though she was crippled and always walked with a cane. When she was sitting, she had a box by her chair with material scraps or mending. When Saturday cleaning was done, she was cutting quilt blocks.

Crosses and Losses, 1924
Cotton, 66 × 80
Original quiltmaker: Susan Kauffman Schrock
Owner: Irene Schrock Beckler, Haven
Faith-South Hutchinson, Mennonite Church

"faspa" (lunch) at four so no time was lost in coming to the house to eat. The Turkey red wheat the Russian Mennonites brought with them made Kansas the "breadbasket of the world" and the mile-long elevators near Hutchinson became white sentinels of the plains.

With all that was happening in her world, no wonder the Amish and Mennonite homemaker used quilting as a way to bring some order and serenity into it. She would piece during the summer when she had a few minutes between gardening and canning and then quilt during the winter. Quilting was a way of relaxing, besides supplying the necessary bedcovers for her family.

Quilts provided a touch of beauty in her home. Quilting was also a part of "rest." Most older Mennonite and Amish women still find it very difficult to "just sit"—they need something to do with their hands. If they have nothing to do, it is like wasting time—"An idle mind (hand) is the Devil's workshop." The Mennonite work ethic generally is alive and well.

Kansas has produced an indomitable people and, because of their belief and faith in God, they continue to face adversity in their lives with more than stoicism.

Aunt Sara never married, so when my first mother died, she was able to come and help my dad. I remember Mrs. Nickel was always so glad for company. She'd always be ready to put "faspa" (lunch) on the table.

Log Cabin (Barnraising variation), c. 1915
Cotton, 72 × 82
Original quiltmakers: Sara Duerksen (pieced)
Marie Dirksen Nickel (quilted)
Owner: Eulalia Duerksen Schroeder, Hillsboro
Alexanderwohl, General Conference Mennonite

Peony, 1930
Cotton, 72 × 92
Original quiltmaker: Fannie Fliginger Zimmerman
Owner: Edna Mosier Zimmerman, South Hutchinson
Sterling, Evangelical Mennonite

This quilt was made by my mother-in-law, who was a very ambitious farmwife. She knew the meaning of "to toil in the soil." She was ingenious with her hands and filled her spare time with sewing, piecing quilts and quilting. She had two quilts ready for each grandchild and each one is a prized possession. This peony quilt, made for her grandson, has reverse appliqué for the stems. She was very concerned that his quilt be used only when company came so it would stay clean and be free from great wear.

I graduated from high school in 1934 during the Depression and the Dust Bowl years. It was my job to herd the cattle—we didn't have fences—so each morning I would take the cattle out, bring them in at noon, back out in the afternoon and back again. To help pass the time, I carried a gallon bucket that became my chair. In my "chair," I had material on which I designed a butterfly appliqué for my first quilt.
—Hillsboro (Mennonite Brethren)

Quilting is so relaxing, especially when there is a snowstorm outside.
—McPherson (General Conference Mennonite)

My mother always quilted and my grandmother did, too, especially in the winter time. You pieced in the summer and quilted in the winter.
—South Hutchinson (Mennonite Church)

Reminiscing
Martha Schmidt Goertz

When my parents settled here, there was just high grass, nothing else. When they wanted to neighbor, there weren't any lanes, no trees for familiar sites, only high grass that you could get lost in. So you would tie a rag on here and a little farther on you'd tie another one and finally you would come to your neighbor. Later they planted sunflowers to mark their way so they could follow those. I think that is why Kansas became the "Sunflower State.". . . . I had four sisters and a brother who lived. Peter lived 11 days and then he passed away. Little Marie, she lived only 11 hours and died. Another little girl lived a few minutes. One boy was born after I was married already, but he was stillborn. There were six children born after my youngest sister but they all died. . . . I ran away from a tornado once. I went down to the south 80 where we had the muskmelons and all at once I saw the cloud and there was the funnel on the ground. I ran this way and that way and then it turned away and missed me. I saw it up close. It wasn't a big one, but I felt so helpless when it came. . . . When Grandpa and I got married, we lived in a two-room house for 12 years; two rooms and five children. When I got my washing machine, it was way off in the granary. I went there and carried that whole big washing machine to the house where I did my laundry. When it was done, I cleaned it and carried it back. That is the way we worked. I had to get the water from way down where the windmill was. From there I carried the water to

Rose Plain, 1935
Rayon and cotton crepe, 77 × 87
Original quiltmaker: owner
Owner: Bertha Goertz Schroeder, Goessel
Tabor, General Conference Mennonite

I made this rose quilt, which was a very popular design, before we were married. My husband even put a few stitches in it so he could say that he'd quilted on it, too. It has a wool batt that I bought for 50¢ from the Cornelius Janzens, who raised sheep.

The quilt has some stains on it because we would lay our children on it on Sundays for their naps, and of course during World War II, we couldn't buy rubber panties. One day we were lucky, however, because a weather balloon landed in our field and the authorities only wanted the equipment—we could keep the balloon. That rubber was almost like manna from heaven at that time.

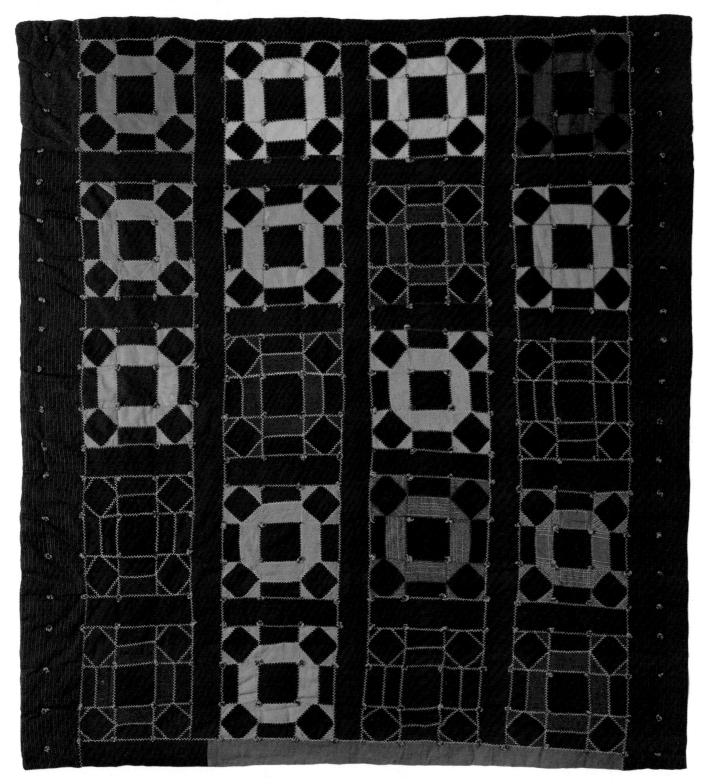

It was winter, during the Depression in 1934, when we lived in Corn, Oklahoma, that I made this comfort. I ripped, washed, and pressed pieces from the old suits of my husband and brother-in-law who were teachers. I also added other wool and warm scraps and tied it with pearl cotton and bunches of colored yarn.

Rolling Stone, 1934
Wools, 72 × 75
Original quiltmaker: Barbara Kleinsasser Wiens Entz
Owner: Marjorie Gerbrandt Wiens, Fresno, California
Parkview, Mennonite Brethren

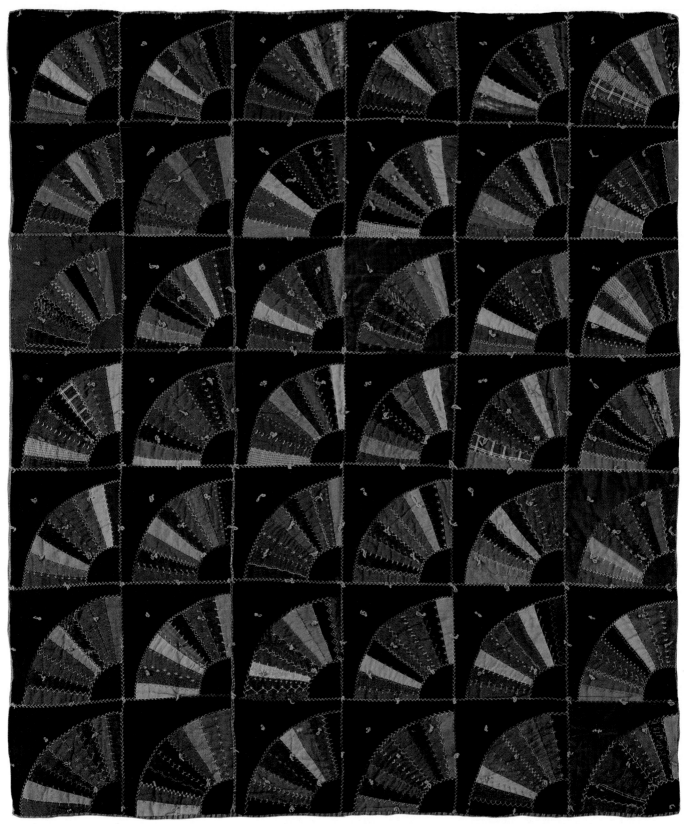

Fan, c. 1910
Wools and rayons, 72 × 97
Original quiltmakers: Susie, Fannie and Cora
Hostetler
Owners: Ralph and Odena Hostetler, Inman
Inman, General Conference Mennonite

This quilt, which my husband inherited, was made by his three maiden aunts who did washing, ironing and sewing to make a living. Making quilts and selling them was also a source of income. Heavy, dark material was used since that was available. Each fan was appliquéd on the block and the design then feather-stitched.

54

the rendering kettle and heated it. . . . And the water was so hard. It always curdled if there was some soap in it. The soap was made of grease and lye and when you washed, those curdles got between the seams. Then when you ironed, it turned to grease. It was terrible. We had to make a big kettle of hot water, put the soap in there and skim it, and then put more soap in. Then it would "break" the water but as soon as you would pour some cold water in there . . . aaach. That wouldn't work. You'd just have to start all over again. . . . [Martha Goertz's daughter, Bertha:] One Monday morning, and Monday was always wash day, we were hanging out the clothes and it was windy. With six children and two adults, there was always a big wash. The clothesline was filled, and because it was so very windy, Mom draped the bigger things and the white Sunday tablecloths over the garden fence so that the wind wouldn't whip them so badly. Then we noticed what we thought was a thunderstorm coming up out of the west. It came so fast and when it got there, it wasn't a thunderstorm—it was a dust storm. The wind and the dust blew so horribly that we had to light the kerosene lamps so we could see in the house. We ran out to get our wash, but the wind had blown the dust, and it was sort of a reddish dust, into the material so tightly that it took two or three washings before they were white again. The dust was just ground into the material. . . .

Reminiscing
Martha
Schmidt
Goertz

Family Ties

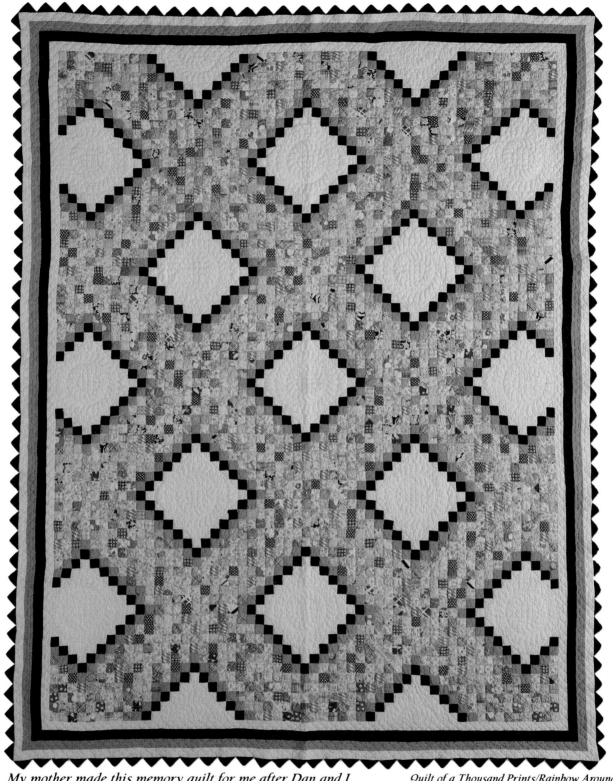

My mother made this memory quilt for me after Dan and I announced our engagement when we were students at Bethel College. She told me I was going to take my family with me and not forget "whence I came." She was a very good seamstress, so I didn't know what it was to have a boughten dress or coat until I was grown. There were five of us children in the family, so she used scraps from shirts, pajamas, dresses or anything else. That was how she was sending memories of my family with me when I left home.

Quilt of a Thousand Prints/Rainbow Around the World, 1934
Cotton, 74 × 94
Original quiltmaker: Selinde Wedel Goering
Owner: Lorena Goering Goering, Moundridge
Eden, General Conference Mennonite

Ohio Star, 1894
Cotton, 73 × 91
Original quiltmaker: Sarah Tice Headings
Owner: Barbara Helmuth Yoder, Hutchinson
Plainview, Conservative Mennonite

This quilt was made by my grandmother for my mother before she got married. I don't know why, but she didn't use the same color thread. Some is stitched with white and some with black.

Grandmother was very much of a quilt lady. Every time we visited her, she'd have another new quilt top ready.

We always enjoyed going to our grandparents' place and were tickled to see them come to ours with their horse and buggy. They had a buggy that was different than others—it was easier to get into than other buggies.

When an older Mennonite or Amish couple considers building or buying a new home, one primary concern will be if the dining room is large enough to seat all the children and grandchildren around the table. There will be plenty of occasions for that because, besides Sunday dinners, there will be lots of holidays to celebrate (some not usually observed by the larger society, like Pentecost and Ascension Day).

The family is all important. Shared meals are tangible evidence of the love families feel for each other. Because Amish and Mennonites generally do not find it easy to verbally express their love for their children, the grandmother will instead prepare her children's and grandchildren's favorite dishes. Then, long after dinner is eaten, often-hilarious conversation continues as the family lingers around the table, telling stories on family members or recounting the week's activities.

Extended family gatherings are also very important. Holidays are celebrated with each side of the family, providing an intergenerational spirit. The young learn to respect all ages.

The Amish naturally have this intergenerational tie because when the parents reach retirement age, they do not leave the farm but build or move into a house next door to their home place, called the "Grossdaadi Haus," or "grandfather house." This allows the younger generation independence, with intergenerational involvement. Many grandmothers babysit while mothers are busy with homemaking. A delightful grandmother near Yoder has a traffic sign in her driveway warning, "Caution, children playing," because her grandchildren spend so much time at her house.

In a traditionally closed society, such as in the Amish or Mennonite churches, parents sought to teach their moral and ethical values to their children, including the belief that there is beauty in neatness and order. Mothers taught their daughters to quilt at an early age with particular quilting patterns and designs sometimes identifying which family had made a quilt. My Grandmother Goertz's favorite pattern was the Carpenter's Wheel, and she made many quilts using it.

Quilts often tied generations together. Because many scraps were shared within the extended family, clothing from as many as three or four generations could be found in one quilt. A patch would be pointed out by one person to another and a story told about the time or the person that scrap represented. Oral history was preserved and passed on.

Quilts were and are lovingly made and passed on as a symbol of the love the maker has for her family. Not only quilts are inherited. Especially in the Amish tradition, glassware is handed down. Brilliant cut glass in a myriad of colors is displayed prominently where it can catch the sunshine. Treasured plates hang on the walls in the more liberal Amish and in Mennonite homes.

Going to family quiltings, which kept families joined, often provided entertainment for them, and still does. Children looked forward to the day as much as the adults did, because they would play with cousins, often under that marvelous tent, the quilt in the frame.

One woman from Whitestone Mennonite Church continues to go quilting with her sisters about once a week and says, "I don't know how we do it, but we quilt about as fast as we talk."

Maintaining that family relationship, especially when miles separate members, is of primary importance. An Inman woman, because she

My grandma pieced a Log Cabin for everyone in the family, for all the children and all the grandchildren. It was literally pieced from scraps she found anywhere. I appreciate it even more now after she has gone through double cataract surgery. We visited her one time after the surgery and she remarked about the colors around. I didn't realize how little she could see and how close to blind she was when she was still working on those Log Cabins.
—Inman (General Conference Mennonite)

Original design (doll quilt), 1952
Cotton, 21 × 28
Original quiltmaker: Sarah Block Priebe
Owner: Jolene Klaassen Stoesz, Los Angeles,
California
Ebenfeld, Mennonite Brethren

**Sara Prieb made this quilt as a
gift for her new twin grandchildren,
Douglas and Jolene.**

cherishes her family, enjoys quilting with her four sisters who live in Iowa. So when she has completed a top, she travels north—"Oh, what a time we have visiting and quilting!"

Keeping family relationships straight can be a puzzle within the Mennonite and Amish churches. (The mailman must almost become an authority on genealogy in some communities because of so many similar names!) People have found one solution to the problem of intermarriage and a limited number of surnames. Within the Amish community, if you speak of someone who shares a name with someone else, you use her husband's name first, such as "Abe Katie" and "Joe Katie." In the area around Goessel where the Russian Mennonites settled, a physical characteristic helps provide the designation, such as "Langa Valter Schmedt" (Tall Walter Schmidt).

Quilting can also serve more than one purpose. In April each year, the Mennonite Central Committee has a "relief sale" in Hutchinson, including a quilt auction. One family from Eden has traditionally made a quilt for that auction together, including cutting the blocks, setting them together and quilting, all as a family. Originally there were five daughters and the mother but now it has extended to granddaughters, granddaughters-in-law, sisters-in-law and even great-granddaughters. The mother and one of the sisters has died, but quilting has bound them together as a family for a purpose and provided a pleasurable, continuing relationship. What more could a family ask?

This quilt was made for my father, W. T. Yoder, before his
marriage, by his mother who lived in Shipshewana, Indiana, and is
dated March 22, 1904. It was tradition that even the young men would
have at least one quilt from home before they got married.

The white is of unbleached muslin and the blue is what used to be
called "Amish blue." My mother always kept the quilt since it was made
for my dad.

Remember featherticks? When we'd go to Ohio to visit relatives,
we used to have a joke about the Ohio beds. One man said that when
he took his wife back to visit, he'd have to help her up into the bed
because of the big, thick featherticks. Then he would get back a
distance and take a running jump into the bed.

Ocean Waves, dated March 22, 1904
Cotton, 66 × 86
Original quiltmaker: Mary Ann Troyer Yoder
Owner: Ruth Yoder Troyer, Hutchinson
Faith-South Hutchinson, Mennonite Church

Blue and Lavendar Plain, 1933
Cotton sateen, 66 × 88
Original quiltmaker: Rosa Schrock Nisly
Owner: Mattie Yoder Nisly, Hutchinson
Amish

My husband's mother made this quilt for him when we got married. She made a quilt for each of her children.

Goose-in-the-Pond, c. 1920
Cotton, 70 × 88
Original quiltmaker: owner
Owner: Lydia Schrock Schrock, Haven
Old Order Amish

My mother gave me scraps for this quilt before I was married. I don't remember where the pink would have come from except that a peddler from Shipshewana, Indiana, would come around, and perhaps she got the material from him.

Pinwheel, 1958
Cotton, 77 × 97
Original quiltmaker: Edna Miller Borntrager
Owner: Wilma Borntrager Beachy, Hutchinson
Amish

Mother made this quilt before we got married. She made a second one like it but said she would never make another one. She was very much of a perfectionist and the points had to be absolutely correct. You see there is yellow in the quilt. Young girls would wear yellow, but after they married, they would wear colors that were more matronly.

I was probably about 13 when I learned to quilt. I began on a border marked with the usual fan pattern. Before that, I remember picking up the pieces from the floor for Mom, one row at a time, and giving them to her to sew together.

—Plainview (Conservative Mennonite)

I have a quilt my mother made years and years ago, maybe 50. She was making such tiny, tiny blocks that she got discouraged and fired it into the corner, where it lay for two days. Then she came back and finished it.

When they quilted it, the nieces came and quilted it. In the evening they had a quilting party where the boys would come. In those days, they spread newspapers on the quilt and then they put the family cat on it. They would call, "Here, kitty, kitty, kitty!" Wherever the kitty ran, that was the next one to be married. It was called "Shaking the Cat."

—Eden (General Conference Mennonite)

My grandmother had 21 grandchildren and when she passed away she had enough quilt tops started for each one of us. Her sisters put the quilt tops in paper bags and numbered them. Then all of us grandchildren picked a number and we got the corresponding quilt. No top was alike and she had used flour sacks for a lot of the quilts.

—Faith-South Hutchinson (Mennonite Church)

Lone Star, 1935
Cotton, 90 × 90
Original quiltmaker: owner
Owner: Olga Woelk Franz, Newton
First-Newton, General Conference Mennonite

I made this quilt before we got married. I hadn't gotten enough material of one color—I needed 1½ yards more. The original material was from Penney's, called Peter Pan, which I had bought for 25¢ a yard, but the additional material was going to cost 29¢. I really debated whether I wanted to pay that much more. I pieced it but it was quilted with my mother and sister helping. It is finished off with hem-stitching and crocheting around the edges.

My husband enlarged the Carpenter's Wheel for me to make this quilt as a gift for our grandson. It uses the colors of Kansas University, where he is a student.

Carpenter's Wheel, 1983
Polyester cotton, 84 × 101
Original quiltmaker: owner
Owner: Irene Stucky Kaufman, McPherson
McPherson, General Conference Mennonite

Gift of Love

My father wanted to give a quilt to my mother, so he asked me to make it. I did all the appliqué and my father gave me $10 for quilting it, which I thought was very good pay in those days.

Ohio Rose, 1933
Cotton, 78 × 96
Original quiltmaker: owner
Owner: Anna Regier Bartel, Hillsboro
Hillsboro, Mennonite Brethren

Generally speaking, most Mennonites and Amish are reserved and probably are not a "hugging" people. They find it difficult to physically demonstrate their love for another, so they find a more concrete way to show it. A quilt is a perfect way to say "I love you."

It is tradition in many families within all the branches to give newly-weds at least one quilt, very likely more. In years past it was the obligation of the bride's mother to provide the bedding for the marriage which included, in some cases, the wedding quilt, a number of comforts, all the sheets and pillowcases, at least two duck pillows and a summer quilt. The Amish mother very often presented the bride with more quilts and the groom usually got at least one quilt from home, which his mother made with his sisters helping.

Within the communities of the Russian-descended Mennonites, two designs were particularly popular as plain wedding quilts, the rose and the waterlily. The future bride took great pride in stitching the quilt herself. It was said that when she began "seeing" a young man, it was time for her to begin her wedding quilt.

Setting up housekeeping at any time is no small matter but at the end of the Depression, it was extremely difficult. My mother remembers:

"I got one cow from home. Your father got two dozen hens, one set of harness and a wagon. He also got an old pie safe that had almost no varnish on it—it had almost been washed off—and the table we used for 28 years from his Grandmother Schroeder and Aunt Susie.

"With the $280 I saved from two years of teaching, I bought a new

This friendship quilt was designed by Maria Stucky Goering in 1928. Embroidered and quilted by the women of Huffnungsfeld Sewing Society, it was given as a token of love to Reverend and Mrs. Gustav Enss when they left that church.

The six center blocks have the Lord's Prayer in German, embroidered by Frieda, Maria's granddaughter. The remaining blocks have the signatures and birthdates of the women of the church.

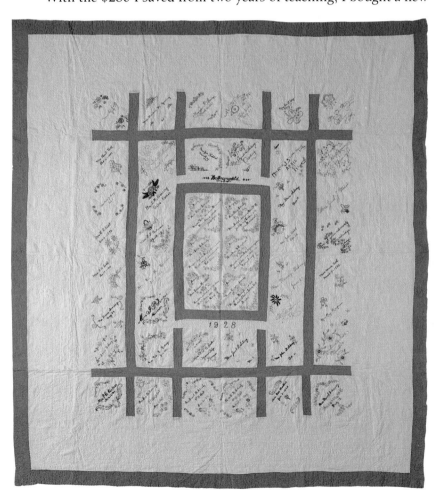

Friendship/Presentation quilt, 1928
Cotton, 70 × 79
Original quiltmaker: Maria Stucky Goering
Owner: Floriene Kaufman Wedel, Moundridge
Eden, General Conference Mennonite

This quilt was made before we moved from Indiana. My mother used scraps from the family sewing. She also made three quilts apiece for her 15 children and, if asked, would help with additional quilts.

Ocean Waves, 1934
Cotton, 70 × 80
Original quiltmaker: Barbara Burkholder Yoder
Owner: Mattie Yoder Nisly, Hutchinson
Amish

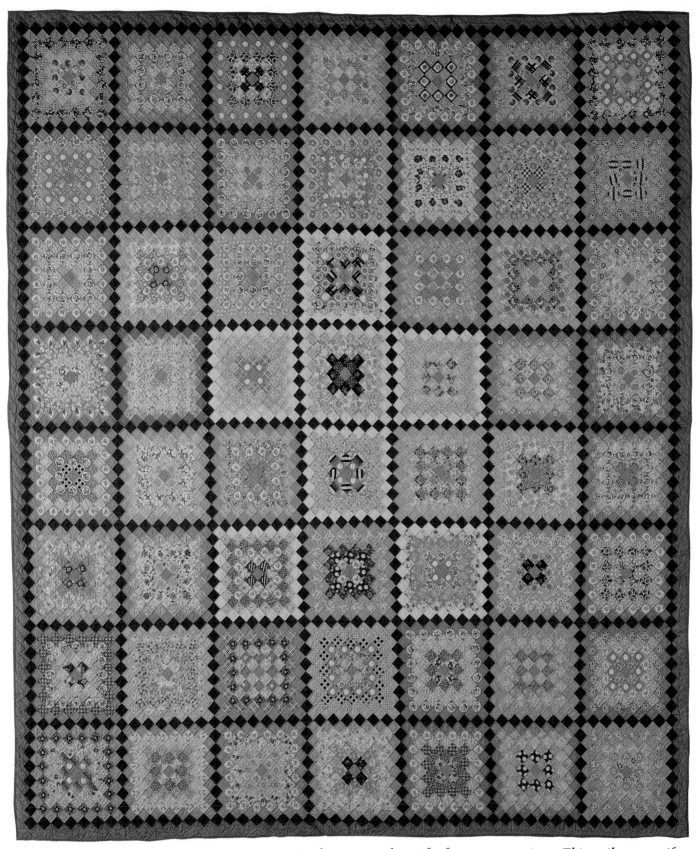

Many Trips Around the World, 1945
Cotton, 78 × 90
Original quiltmaker: Anna Loucks Bowen
Owners: Perry and Florence Johnson, Galva
Lone Tree, Holdeman

Quilts were used as gifts for many occasions. This quilt was a gift from my husband's aunt. We visited her in her home in Hesston shortly after our marriage and she let us choose a quilt from several she had on hand. Being just new in the family, I hesitated and, since she was my husband's aunt, I let him choose. She let us know later it was her favorite quilt, but she felt proud that we cherished it.

Unknown design (similar to Ferris Wheel), 1911
Cotton, 75 × 88
Original quiltmaker: Mary Holdeman Loucks
Owners: Perry and Florence Johnson, Galva
Lone Tree, Holdeman

For some reason, perhaps because she liked to piece quilts, my husband's grandmother promised her girls for every year they didn't marry after reaching the age of 21, she'd make them a quilt. My husband's mother, Samantha Unruh Johnson, married at 27, so she got seven quilts from her mother.

After her three sons married, Samantha still had three unused quilts (I'm sure she saved them purposely) and gave them to us for Christmas in 1971.

bed, a dresser, sewing machine, a wardrobe, 6 chairs, a 3-burner oil stove with an oven you could lift off, a wood range, a cream separator, a kitchen cabinet that I paid 75¢ for. I also bought one heifer due to freshen soon, a rake and hoe. Herb bought a Twin City tractor on time and a drill for $20 that had to be dug out of the dust in Western Kansas."

Quilts, of course, were not only used to celebrate a marriage, but friendship. Friends embroidered their names on blocks, maybe including the year or their birthdates, set the blocks together, stitched the quilt and gave it to one of their friends. Sometimes a family friendship quilt was made with the mother's name embroidered in the center of the quilt. Friendship quilts have gone through several periods of popularity in the 1930s, the 1950s, and are seeing a revival again.

Because the church played such an important part in the life of the Mennonites, quilts also were used to demonstrate that tie. Instead of the usual friendship quilts, making a quilt with all the names of the members of the baptismal class embroidered on it was popular for a period of time.

Special quilts recognizing the contribution that a person had made to various lives were popular and continue to be. Teachers received them fairly regularly, even from the school district parents in one case. A well-loved school and camp cook received quilts, proving the adage that the "way to the heart is through the stomach."

The presentation quilt, a style of friendship quilt, was often given to a pastor, when he left one church for another, as a "token of love." A plain quilt or a quilt with blocks portraying events out of a couple's life together is now frequently given to parents celebrating a significant anniversary. A quilt is also given to a couple when they move from one community to another, all a testimony to their friends' affection.

Perhaps the nicest surprise of all is when a quilt is given for no special reason, just because a person is loved. One woman remembers when she was a young girl, her mother received a package from the mother's sister in Nebraska. She can remember seeing her mother sitting and crying after opening the package to find a beautiful Flower Garden quilt—it was such a marvelous thing that her sister had done for her.

Husbands have found a way to also become a part of this kind of gift giving. Two couples in Hillsboro make plain quilts for their grandchildren and the husbands' stitches are as neat as the wives'. Another husband does the dishes and cleans the house when his wife has a quilt in so she does not have to take time out for the ordinary.

For many Mennonites and Amish, giving a tangible gift of love is not the most important gift they can give their children. They feel the greatest gift is to guide them toward their acceptance of the "Lord Jesus Christ as their personal Savior." When a child does become a Christian, they feel the most important aspect of their childrearing has been accomplished. They recall with thanksgiving another gift, "For God so loved the world that he gave his only begotten son . . ." (John 3:16).

An elderly lady in our Illinois congregation was disposing of her things and gave this crazy patch to the women's group, who often gave quilts and comforts away to the needy. This quilt, however, was not suitable for that. Since we were the new parsonage family, we were given this quilt as a friendly gesture.

Crazy Patch, c. 1900
Silks, satins, crepe, 62 × 62
Original quiltmaker: unknown
Owner: Eunice Gingerich Histand, Hesston Whitestone, Mennonite Church

The Quilting Community

I got the idea for this quilt from Capper's Weekly *but put it together differently. The back is plain feed sack. At that time we used what we had—nothing was bought unless absolutely necessary.*

Quilting in those days was always a much-looked-forward-to time. All the aunts and cousins would come for the day and there would be lots of visiting with a big noon meal.

Single Wedding Ring, 1953
Cotton, 75 × 90
Original quiltmaker: Edna Nisly Yoder
Owner: Esther Yoder, Hutchinson
Plainview, Conservative Mennonite

Years ago, the quilting party, besides being an important social event, served as the radio and newspaper of the day. It was also the first informal support group for women.

The quilting group continues the latter function for many women. It helps them deal with crises in their lives, particularly death, since many of the quilters are older. A number of them have commented, "I don't know what I would have done if I couldn't have come here and quilted after my husband died."

In larger Mennonite churches, where learning to know every member well is virtually impossible, the quilting program serves as a woman's caring community. At many Amish and Mennonite quiltings, women discuss raising children and grandchildren, farm problems, health, death and faith issues. They share news about extended family members living in other communities and states.

A quilting is also a way to train the next generation. Often a "learner's quilt" is set up and the more experienced members will help a younger person learn the art. Never would anyone think of removing any of those longish stitches, because that would diminish the learner's self-esteem—"The quilt will hold together."

The Mennonites and Amish were, however, also taught not to be "puffed up" with pride. Numerous scriptures reinforced this, including Proverbs 16:5, 18: "Everyone that is proud in heart is an abomination to the Lord" and "Pride goeth before a fall"; and Matthew 6:3: "Let not thy left hand know what thy right hand doeth." While excessive pride is still considered a serious character flaw, quilting apparently provides an avenue for a legitimate display of the quilter's activity.

Stories are told about years ago when Amish and the more conservative Mennonite quilters did not use white thread because that would have been considered too "fancy" or "worldly." Only black thread was to be used, because then the stitches would not be as obvious on the dark material and the quilter would not be too proud of her tiny, uniform stitches. Within several Mennonite branches, tradition also required the quiltmaker to make an obvious error to demonstrate her humility—only God was perfect.

Usually enough women will be invited to a quilting to "fill the whole quilt"—each side is covered. A quilting will be planned for the entire day. If a member without children isn't there by 8 a.m., she is late. The women plan a big dinner, and certainly one of the "entertainments" for the day is eating. New recipes are tested, evaluated and exchanged.

There is almost a jostling for position at the quiltings. Good-natured kidding will take place about one quilter not wanting to sit next to another because one is too fast and will be ready to "roll" before the other is ready. A woman who otherwise might not consider her left-handedness a special gift will be "honored" at a quilting with the corners.

Conversations around the quilt take place in a variety of dialects sprinkled with English: Pennsylvania Dutch, Swiss German and Low German. For many, English is their second language.

Many Mennonite groups often quilt for others, to raise money for relief or to fund their own missionary causes. This is where older members can still feel useful. Individual members also do quilting in their homes to earn money, sometimes still called "egg money" (farmwives used to earn money by selling eggs from their small flocks of

This was a quilt I planned with my mother's help before we were married. The Bethel College Quilters, who have been quilting since around 1917, did the quilting. Many of the quilters were my mother's personal friends and I was acquainted with them all. Some were my former Sunday school teachers or mothers of my friends. I was able to put an "H" in the center of the quilt since I was marrying a Hiebert, making the quilt reversible.

Plain, 1937
Cotton sateen, 80 × 93
Original quiltmaker: owner
Owner: Elizabeth Penner Hiebert Brandt, Newton
Bethel College, General Conference Mennonite

The Disk, 1905
Cotton, 72 × 72
Original quiltmaker: Elizabeth Schrock (pieced)
Amanda Hochstetler Schrock
(quilted)
Owner: Judith Schrock Miller, Hutchinson
Beachy Amish

Elizabeth Schrock, who was eleven years old, was unable to go to school because of severe heart disease. During her illness, she would often sit on the porch and piece quilt tops from scraps from the family sewing as well as using pieces contributed by community people. Elizabeth died the year after she completed this top. Her mother, Amanda Hochstetler Schrock, stitched the completion date, May 14, 1928, into the quilt.

chickens).

Because quilting is such an integral part of life for so many Amish and Mennonites and a quilt is virtually always up, it can be in the way when the family comes over. For some quilters, making room is not a big job because ropes and special hooks screwed into the ceiling hold the frame and quilt up there until quilting can begin again. Children of Old Order Amish quilters have given their mothers specially-adapted butane lamps, which resemble a floor lamp with the filament at the top of the post, so the quilter will be able to quilt at night.

Two quilting groups, the Bethesda Home Quilters in Goessel and the Bethel College Mission Quilters in North Newton, incorporate a unique feature. Readers will spend about 1½ hours each time they meet reading a book or an article of special interest. No one knows why this practice began but perhaps it was a way to prevent gossip or, because Mennonites emphasized not wasting time and only the fingers were busy, listening was a way of being frugal.

Leaving a group and no longer quilting is very difficult for many women. It is done only when health demands it or eyesight dims. One woman, who experienced the break in quilting, observed, "Quilting is about as hard to give up as driving a car."

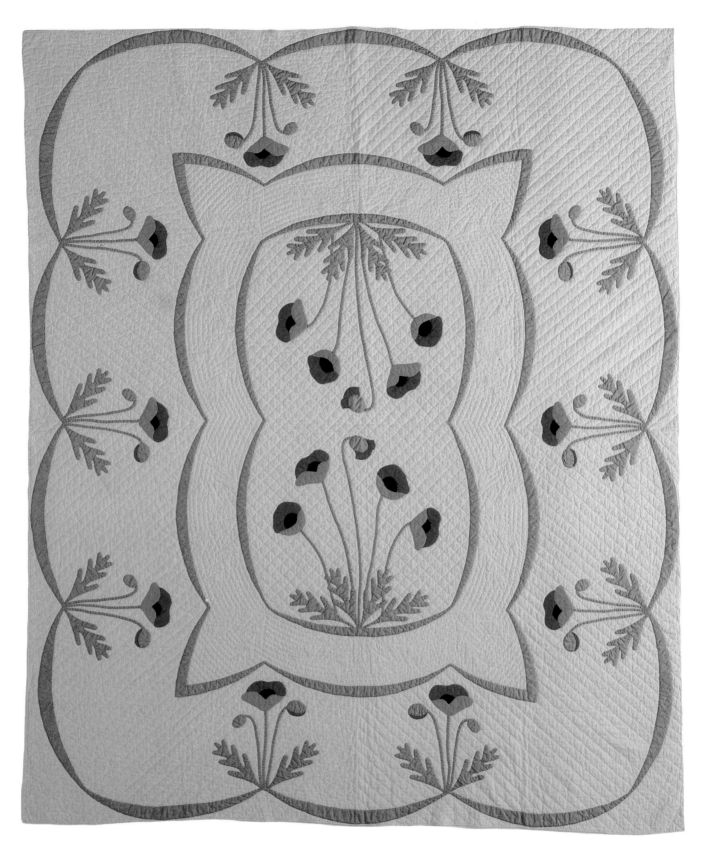

This quilt was made by my mother-in-law during the polio years. Her twelve-year-old daughter, Elva Mae, had polio and it was after her hospitalization that Edna made this quilt. The handiwork was mental therapy for her.

Poppies, 1947
Cotton, 72 × 84
Original quiltmaker: Edna Harder Suderman
Owners: Art and Harriet Klaassen Suderman, Hillsboro
Ebenfeld, Mennonite Brethren

My mother can't see very well. She just can't quilt anymore and it is very hard on her, but she brings her needle threader and keeps our needles threaded. That way she is still a part of the group here.

—Plainview (Conservative Mennonite)

I can't quilt anymore—I have a problem with my right hand, so I learned to embroider with my left. I keep coming every Thursday with my embroidery when the rest are quilting because this is where I want to be. This is where I am cared for.

—McPherson (General Conference Mennonite)

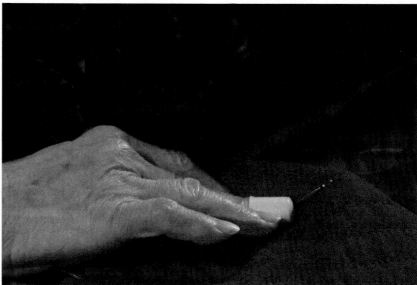

Why do I keep coming to quilt here at church? You know, at the age of 82 or 83, it is a way to feel useful, and I love the fellowship.

—Bethel College (General Conference Mennonite)

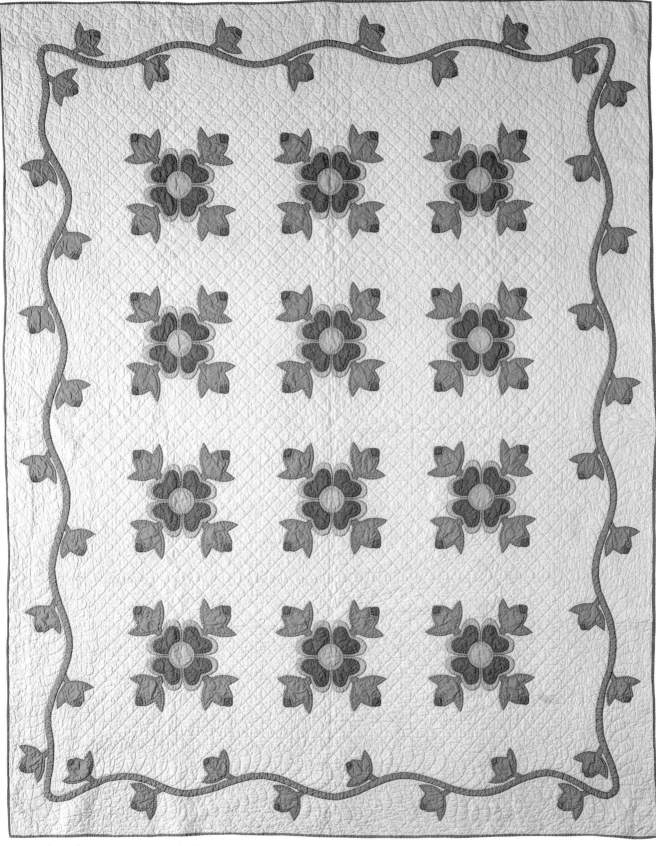

This Ohio Rose was made by my mother-in-law, but a good friend of hers helped piece the top. Her friend was bedfast at the time and this helped her pass the time. The pieces are appliquéd with a black running stitch.

Ohio Rose, c. 1925
Cotton, 69 × 85
Original quiltmaker: Katherine Toews Schierling
Owners: Ben and Minnie Hahn Schierling, Inman
Inman, General Conference Mennonite

Plain original design, 1954
Cotton, 80 × 99
Original quiltmaker: Minnie Lehrman Unruh
Owner: Evelyn Unruh Schmidt, Canton
Alexanderwohl, General Conference Mennonite

My mother designed and quilted this quilt and gave it to us as a Christmas surprise. She has done a lot of quilting, quilt marking and designing in her 91 years. It began as a hobby but became a way of earning money because her unique gift became well known. She was written up in the March 1980 issue of the Quilter's Newsletter. *She began the Bethesda Quilters in Goessel, a very active quilting group, which quilts to raise money for the Home there.*

Flower Basket Appliqué, 1938
Cotton, 80 × 95
Original quiltmaker: owner
Owner: Edna Penner Fast, Hillsboro
Hillsboro, Mennonite Brethren

The YMCA organization at Tabor College in Hillsboro would sponsor a mission sale once a year. The college girls would make a few quilts and embroider various items to sell at that time.

I embroidered and appliquéd this quilt while I was a student at Tabor. The quilting was done by the wives of the Tabor faculty, including the wife of the college president.

Original design appliqué, 1936
Cotton, 72 × 90
Original quiltmakers: Hilda, Norma and Irene Schmidt
Owner: Hilda Schmidt Schmidt, Lehigh
Lehigh, General Conference Mennonite

My sisters, Norma and Irene, and I designed this quilt. Whenever we would go visiting someplace, other people had quilts so we thought we would like to have one, too. We made up the kind of flowers, drew them and then appliquéd them. We put up the quilt in the front room and we had a quilting party with friends and neighbors.

Precious Memories

My mother so loved to quilt. She found many, many patterns in the Kansas City Star. *She'd often use those patterns to make sample blocks and stored them away for future use. I still have that box—it's filled with memories.*

Double sawtooth with edges forming Wild Goose Chase, c. 1940
Cotton, 85 × 87
Original quiltmaker: Mattie Nissley Keim
Owner: Emma Keim, Haven
Old Order Amish

Stars and Blocks, 1939
Cotton, 75 × 86
Original quiltmaker: Mary Miller Yoder
Owner: Abe Yoder, Hutchinson
Amish

This quilt is one I got from home before we married, and my sister helped my mother quilt it. It's small, but then our beds were small, too. I had a rope bed and we had either straw or cornhusk ticks. Times have really changed.

Red was used a lot. I remember there was a lot of red furniture in my grandparents' home, maybe because that had been popular in Ohio where my family originally came from. They had a red bureau, desk, cupboard, chairs, highchair and a red woodbox that was always behind the stove. We now have one of the chairs and the highchair.

A quilt is not just a quilt. It is not an inanimate object only to be spread on a bed or hung on a wall. It is the repository of special memories associated with a well-loved individual. It is a time recalled—an event of huge proportions such as a birth or death, or the hardly earthshaking memory of having the children use it as a tent over the card table. A quilt is not just a quilt.

A quilt is a hug, chicken soup and a pat on the back. It is comfort.

A quilt is tradition—mothers giving quilts to children and the children giving quilts to *their* children.

A quilt is courage. A quilter recalls with affection, whenever she feels there is something she cannot accomplish on her own, how Aunt Mathilda, confined to a wheelchair, was able to single-handedly put in a quilt. Somehow she was able to stretch it out and pin it into the frame. Remembering Aunt Mathilda, the quilter gathers courage to do what needs to be done.

A quilt is feed sacks, a patch on top of a patch. It is hard times, little money, tears, a sale of cattle to help pay off debts. It covers a person who is ill. It is death and sadness.

It is a grandmother making her granddaughter feel very special by assigning an area on a Double Wedding Ring quilt for her where she will do the stitching. The grandmother then marks that spot with a piece of material basted to the quilt on which the little girl has signed, "Erica, age 7."

A quilt is a crazy patch made of neckties where a sister's brothers will stay forever young.

A quilt is springtime, the smell of clean clothes and all the family's quilts flying from the clothesline.

A quilt is time suspended. Friends and family who signed a friendship quilt are still all together, alive in warm friendship. It is a time when difficulties have not divided friends in a church, but all are united where nothing will separate them.

A quilt is the reminder of the love of a mother for her nine children when she embroidered a quilt for each of them and pieced a quilt for her 22 grandchildren.

A quilt is an "Oh, yahmer" when you see how much work has gone into the making and stitching of such a marvelous gift of love.

A Carpenter's Wheel quilt is Grandma Goertz, her perfect and luscious butterscotch pies, bright, shiny wooden floors, the ticking of the mantel clock and the south wind whistling through the screens of her side porch.

A quilt is new romance, a handsome young man, a Model T car. A wedding, the first home, the birth of a child.

A Sunday quilt is family gatherings, jokes and laughter, Christmas sacks, *pluma moos,* grandparents' joy, the pleasure of being together.

A quilt is a mother teaching a daughter how to cut and piece a quilt, sitting at her side as she treadles away. It is a mother being patient with the long stitches and not removing them.

A quilt is a reminder of our ancestors who, because of their faith in God's guidance, had courage to strike out for new lands without knowing what awaited them. From the diary of Jacob Schmidt, my great-great-grandfather:

"August 23, 1874: At 10 a.m. a committee of six left for the State of Kansas. Friday afternoon we went to Lincoln and bought cooking

stoves at $38 a piece.

"September 6: Friday at 1 p.m. our delegation returned from Kansas. The land is good, wells are 100 feet deep or more. Between the land and railroad there are sandhills 4 miles long and deep valleys. The president of the railroad company promises us so much, it's almost unbelievable. Wants us to settle down there.

"September 7: Saturday evening it was decided *that we go to Kansas.*"

My Amish grandmother pieced the top which we found in a trunk that had pieces of cedar wood in it to help preserve it. It is made of cotton sateen, which was very popular, and the blue is called "Amish blue." Her hands were always busy. Part of it is pieced by machine and some by hand. Apparently, when she went somewhere or when it wasn't convenient to be by the machine, she'd piece by hand. It probably is the last quilt she pieced.

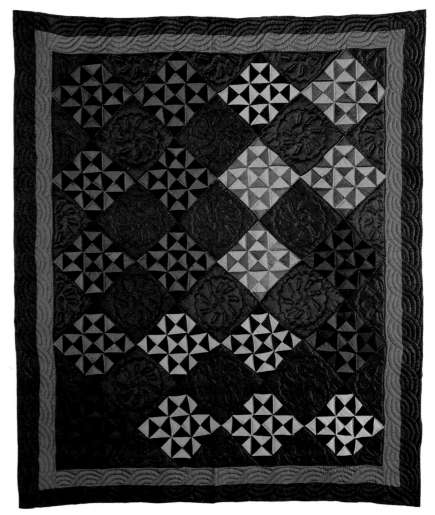

Broken Dishes, 1948
Cotton sateen, 72 × 85
Original quiltmakers: Susan Kauffman Schrock
(pieced)
Owner, Edna Troyer
Schrock (quilted)
Owner: Irene Schrock Beckler, Haven
Faith-South Hutchinson, Mennonite Church

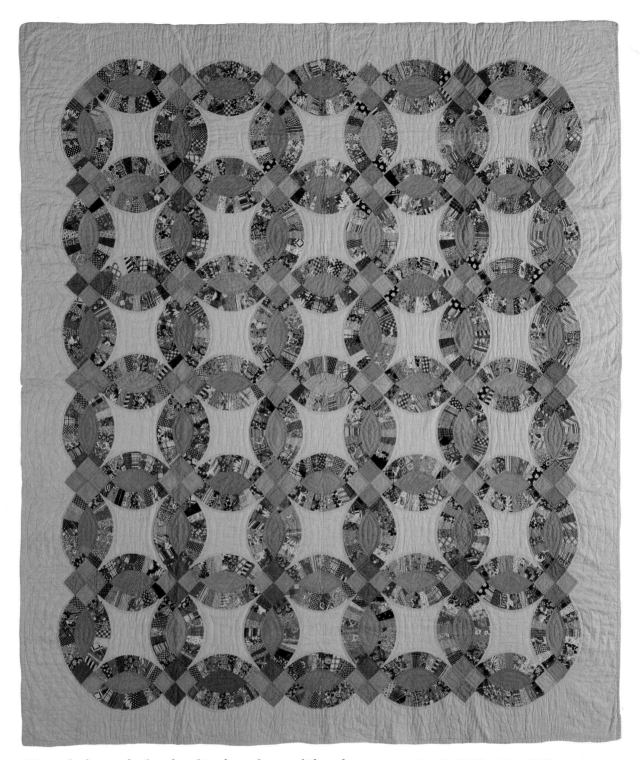

We used what we had on hand in those days and then, because we needed orchid and yellow, we dyed feed sacks to get that. Mother pieced the top by hand because she had an enlarged heart and couldn't pedal the sewing machine. This was the last quilt she pieced.

My future husband and I wanted to get married, but my mother had asked that I take care of her until her death. My father said that the only way we could be married was if we lived with them, so for almost a year we lived at home with my parents. My father said I certainly deserved this quilt top and after he remarried, my stepmother asked if she could quilt it for me.

Double Wedding Ring, 1944
Cotton, 80 × 95
Original quiltmakers: Sara Wiens Martin (pieced)
                                    Anna Vogt Martin (quilted)
Owner: Esther Martin Funk, Lehigh
Lehigh, General Conference Mennonite

Sunbonnet Sue, 1928
Cotton, 96 × 96
Original quiltmakers: owner (pieced)
                          Sadie Byler White (quilted)
Owner: Elsie White, Hesston
Hesston College, Mennonite Church

Quilting really isn't limited to being a woman's art. I have a quilt that is very dear to me. When my father had his heart attack, he was told not to do any manual labor, so he bought a sewing machine and he went to work and appliquéd quilt tops. Each of us kids has a top that he appliquéd and Mother quilted. It is a real precious thing to me.
—*Alexanderwohl (General Conference Mennonite)*

Everyone used to have a Crazy Patch, and beautiful ones, too. They would use wools and silks and embroider around the blocks with various stitches. Silk was a lot more plentiful then because most of our grandmas had black silk dresses for church. And cashmere.
—*Eden (General Conference Mennonite)*

I have an old quilt that I treasure, made of patches of material from when I was a little girl in the 1930s. My mother cut them out and I remember sewing them together by hand. I remember the chocolate box that I kept them all in. And then after I married, my mother put it together and sent it to me for my birthday.
—*Inman (General Conference Mennonite)*

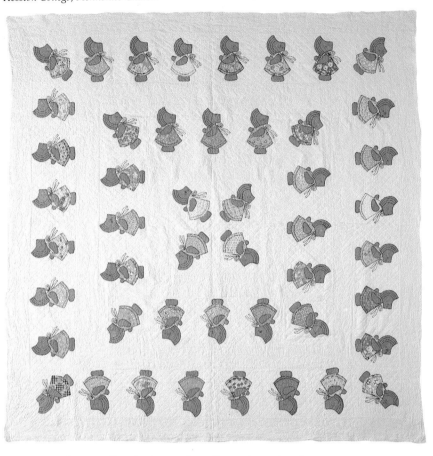

A quilt isn't finished in a day. Sometimes it takes years.

I began making this quilt in 1928 when I was eleven years old. Our grade school was a one-room school. When it was too cold to go outside to play during recess, our teacher encouraged the girls to do embroidery work.

I got the pattern from a friend who attended school with me. I worked on the quilt off and on for 12 years until it was finally finished, when my mother quilted it.

Some of the fabric is 56 years old because I got the pink and blue for the bonnets and arms at one time. The prints are mostly from my sisters' and my dresses that my mother made for us over the years. Some fabrics were from my friend's scraps that we traded. In those days, you could send for fabric scraps from the catalog, so I sent for a package and got several of my Sunbonnet Girls' dresses from that bundle.

My Grandmother Heatwole thought little girls should learn to sew by hand so she made a plan to help us. She cut the quilt blocks for us and taught us how to sew them together, which I did when I was five years old. I used scraps from my aprons, which I would wear over my woolen dresses, a red apron one week and a dark blue the next. A Nine-patch was often used to teach young girls how to piece.

So all these years I kept my precious 42 blocks in the cedar chest. Then in 1979, with the help of my sister-in-law and a friend, the top was completed. Even though the border and the blue-gray fabric are new, they are like what would have been used during the time the blocks were made. I also quilted it with the fan design that my mother used in her quilts.

Nine-patch, 1917
Cotton and cotton polyester, 90 × 99
Original quiltmaker: owner
Owner: Leah Yoder Loucks, Hesston
Hesston College, Mennonite Church

91

Blazing Star, c. 1910
Cotton, 72 × 80
Original quiltmaker: Emma Headings Yutzy
Owner: Emma Yutzy Miller, Hutchinson
Plainview, Conservative Mennonite

This quilt was made by my Amish grandmother. I'm not sure how some of the colors got in it because they wouldn't have worn them. Perhaps neighbors gave her scraps. The blue they would have worn—wedding dresses were that color.

Grandmother had nine children so she surely had enough scraps. She especially enjoyed making quilts and rugs. She lived to 94, outliving three of her children.

I have a Log Cabin comfort that shows what kind of material was used at least 90 years ago. I think they called it China cotton. My grandmother came from Russia when she was about six years old. My grandmother was sick about the time my mother was born, and they had a "kaeksha," a maid, who helped Grandmother, and that maid pieced these comforts by hand. Where a maid would have found time in those days—she went milking, too—I don't know, but somehow she did and made comforts for the family.

—*Tabor (General Conference Mennonite)*

I started a quilt when I was in my sophomore year in college and the first years of teaching—I had to have something to do besides grading papers, so I started embroidering blocks but only got 20 finished. I put them away and there they stayed until almost our 25th wedding anniversary. All of a sudden my mother asked for them and I gave them to her. So with the help of my sister-in-law, they finished embroidering the rest, pieced it and then the ladies of this church quilted it for our anniversary 15 years ago.

—*Inman (General Conference Mennonite)*

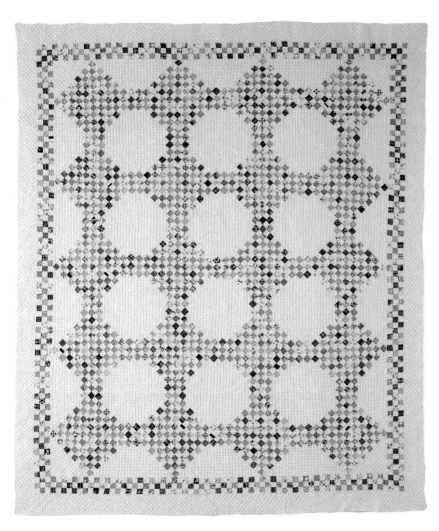

Original design, c. 1960
Cotton, 76 × 90
Original quiltmaker: Mary Winkler Emch
Owner: Bill Emch, Madison
Lamont, Apostolic Christian

Grandmother Emch did housework for others before her marriage and didn't make quilts until after her marriage in 1890. She rarely bought material but used the scraps left after making her children's clothing. She was a wonderful quiltmaker and a beautiful quilter.

She pieced this quilt when she was 90 years old and others helped her quilt it. Grandmother gave it to me when it was finished so it is very special to us.

93

Readings and Sources

About Other Quilts

Beyer, Jinny. *Patchwork Patterns*. McLean, Virginia: EPM Publications, 1979.

Bishop, Robert, and Elizabeth Safanda. *A Gallery of Amish Quilts*. New York: E.P. Dutton & Co., Inc., 1976.

Haders, Phyllis. *The Warner Collector's Guide to American Quilts*. New York: Main Street Press, 1981.

Hall, Carrie A., and Rose G. Kretsinger. *The Romance of the Patchwork Quilt in America*. New York: Bonanza Books, 1935.

Hassel, Carla J. *You Can Be a Super Quilter!* Des Moines: Wallace-Homestead Book Co., 1980.

Khin, Yvonne M. *The Collector's Dictionary of Quilt Names and Patterns*. Washington, D.C.: Acropolis Books, Ltd., 1980.

Leone, Diana. *The Sampler Quilt*. Santa Clara, California: Leone Publications, 1980.

Lithgow, Marilyn. *Quiltmaking and Quiltmakers*. New York: Funk & Wagnall's, 1974.

Nelson, Cyril I., and Carter Houck. *Treasury of American Quilts*. New York: Greenwich House, 1984.

Pellman, Rachel T. *Amish Quilt Patterns*. Intercourse, Pennsylvania: Good Books, 1984.

———, and Kenneth Pellman. *The World of Amish Quilts*. Intercourse, Pennsylvania: Good Books, 1984.

———, and Joanne Ranck. *Quilts Among the Plain People*. Intercourse, Pennsylvania: Good Books, 1981.

General Reading

Braght, Thielman J. van, comp. *The Bloody Theatre, or Martyrs Mirror*. Scottdale, Pennsylvania: Herald Press, 1950.

Cooper, Patricia, and Norma Bradley Buferd. *The Quilters: Women and Domestic Art*. New York: Doubleday & Co., 1977.

Denlinger, A. Martha. *Real People*. Scottdale, Pennsylvania: Herald Press, 1975.

Dyck, Cornelius J. *An Introduction to Mennonite History*. Scottdale, Pennsylvania: Herald Press, 1981.

Good, Merle and Phyllis. *20 Most Asked Questions About the Amish and Mennonites*. Intercourse, Pennsylvania: Good Books, 1979.

Haury, David A. *Prairie People: A History of the Western District Conference*. Newton, Kansas: Faith and Life Press, 1981.

Hostetler, John A. *Mennonite Life*. Scottdale, Pennsylvania: Herald Press, 1983.

Miller, Levi. *Our People: The Amish and Mennonites of Ohio*. Scottdale, Pennsylvania: Herald Press, 1983.

Smith, C. Henry. *The Story of the Mennonites*. Newton, Kansas: Faith and Life Press, 1981.

Stratton, Joanne L. *Pioneer Women: Voices from the Kansas Frontier*. New York: Simon & Schuster, 1981.

More Specific Reading About Various Branches

Apostolic Christian Church History, Vol. 1. Chicago: Apostolic Christian Publishing Co., 1949.

Bender, Harold S., and Smith, C. Henry, eds. *The Mennonite Encyclopedia, Vols. 1–4.* Scottdale, Pennsylvania: Herald Press, and Newton, Kansas: Faith and Life Press, 1955–59.

Good, Merle. *Who Are the Amish?* Intercourse, Pennsylvania: Good Books, 1985.

Hiebert, Clarence: *The Holdeman People: The Church of God in Christ, Mennonite, 1859–1969.* South Pasadena, California: William Carey Library, 1973.

Hostetler, John A. *Amish Life.* Scottdale, Pennsylvania: Herald Press, 1981.

————. *Amish Society.* Baltimore: Johns Hopkins University Press, 1974.

Nussbaum, Stan. *You Must Be Born Again: A History of the Evangelical Mennonite Church.* n.p., 1980.

Pannabecker, Samuel F. *Open Doors: A History of the General Conference Mennonite Church.* Newton, Kansas: Faith and Life Press, 1975.

Penner, John M. *A Concise History of the Church of God* [in Christ, Mennonite—Holdeman]. Moundridge, Kansas: Gospel Publishers, 1978.

Schweider, Elmer, and Dorothy Schweider. *A Peculiar People: Iowa's Old Order Amish.* Ames, Iowa: Iowa State University Press, 1975.

Toews, J. A. *A History of the Mennonite Brethren Church.* Hillsboro, Kansas: Mennonite Brethren Publishing House, 1982.

Wenger, J. C. *The Mennonite Church in America.* Scottdale, Pennsylvania: Herald Press, 1966.

Wiebe, Katie Funk. *Who Are the Mennonite Brethren?* Winnipeg, Manitoba: Kindred Press, 1985.

Wittinger, Carlton O. *Quest for Piety and Obedience: The Story of the Brethren in Christ Church.* Nappanee, Indiana: Evangel Press, 1978.

Zug, Joan Liffring, and the Mennonite Historical Society of Iowa, Inc. *The Kalona Heritage.* Monticello, Iowa: Jilin Printing Co., 1975.

Museums

Kauffman Museum (pioneer and Mennonite life), Highway 15 (across from Bethel College campus entrance), N. Newton, Kansas, 316-283-1612; admission.

Mennonite Heritage Complex (replica of immigrant barracks, Turkey Red Wheat Palace, one-room school, Friesen house), Highway 15, Goessel, Kansas, 316-367-8200; admission.

Pioneer Adobe House and Museum (example of Russian Mennonite house with barn attached), U.S. Highway 56 and Ash, Hillsboro, Kansas, 316-947-3775; donations accepted.

Warkentin House (home of the man who built two mills to grind the Turkey Red hard winter wheat brought by the Russian Mennonites), 211 E. First St., Newton, Kansas, 316-283-3113; admission.

Index

About the Author

Judy Schroeder Tomlonson was born and raised in the Tabor Church (General Conference Mennonite) near Goessel, Kansas, where she learned to love the Mennonites and appreciate their values and beliefs. She attended Bethel College (also General Conference) in N. Newton, Kansas.

Through the influence of her grandmother, Martha Schmidt Goertz, and a patient, helpful mother, Bertha Goertz Schroeder, she has become an avid, prize-winning quilter. Because of her background in art and involvement in her own decorating business, she learned to appreciate what a marvelous piece of art a quilt is.

She lives in Warrensburg, Missouri, where her husband Jim pastors a Church of the Brethren congregation. They have three children: Jana, recently married; Jill, a high school senior; and Jeremy, an eighth grader.